SHOW THEM MY LOVE

Now let me show you a way of life that is best of all

Author

Lorraine A Molyneaux

xulon PRESS

Copyright © 2013 by Lorraine A. Molyneaux

Show Them My Love
by Lorraine A. Molyneaux

Printed in the United States of America

ISBN 9781625099860

All rights reserved solely by the author. The author guarantees all contents are original and do not infringe upon the legal rights of any other person or work. No part of this book may be reproduced in any form without the permission of the author. The views expressed in this book are not necessarily those of the publisher.

Unless otherwise indicated, Bible quotations are taken from The Holy Bible, New Living Translation. Copyright ©1996, 2004 by Tyndale House Publishers Inc., Carol Stream, Illinois.

www.xulonpress.com

CONTENTS

INTRODUCTION vii
DEDICATION ix
ACKNOWLEDGMENTS xi

Chapter 1 - Miracles 13

Chapter 2 - Healings 34

Chapter 3 - Testimonies 46

Chapter 4 - Mission Call to First Nation's – 2008 64

Chapter 5 - RAPID LAKE 67

Chapter 6 - MAIGANAJIK 82

Chapter 7 - My Best Friend Can Be Your Best
              Friend Too 123

Chapter 8 - Scripture Verses (NLT) 129

ABOUT THE AUTHOR 133

INTRODUCTION

This is a collection of stories, journal entries and testimonies about the wonderful goodness of God experienced in daily life. There are testimonies of healings, miracles, casting out demons and raising the dead through faith in the Name of Jesus Christ.

These stories were written by the Author and others who have personally experienced God's miraculous intervention. Also included are reports and updates from mission trips to several First Nation Reservations located in Northern Quebec, Canada.

As you read these testimonies, your faith in God will increase and you will experience the wonderful goodness of God.

Psalm 105:1-5

Give thanks to the Lord and proclaim his greatness. Let the whole world know what he has done. Sing to him; yes, sing his praises. Tell everyone about his wonderful deeds. Exult in his holy name; rejoice, you who worship the Lord. Search for the Lord and for his strength; continually seek him. Remember the wonders he has performed, his miracles, and the rulings he has given, you children of his servant Abraham, you descendants of Jacob, his chosen ones.

DEDICATION

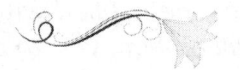

*T*his book was written to honor God and His Son, our wonderful Lord Jesus Christ, to acknowledge His Goodness as revealed through His ever present Holy Spirit, and to give Him praise.

Psalm 145

I will exalt you, my God and King, and praise your name forever and ever. I will praise you every day; yes, I will praise you forever. Great is the Lord! He is most worthy of praise! No one can measure his greatness. Let each generation tell its children of your mighty acts; let them proclaim your power. I will meditate on your majestic, glorious splendor and your wonderful miracles. Your awe-inspiring deeds will be on every tongue; I will proclaim your greatness. Everyone will share the story of your wonderful goodness; they will sing with joy about your righteousness. The Lord is merciful and compassionate, slow to get angry and filled with unfailing love. The Lord is good to everyone. He showers compassion on all his creation. All of your works will thank you, Lord, and your faithful followers will praise you. They will speak of the glory of your kingdom; they will give examples of your power. They will tell about your mighty deeds and about the majesty and glory of your reign. For your kingdom is an everlasting kingdom. You rule throughout all generations. The Lord always keeps his promises; he is gracious in all he does. The Lord helps the fallen and lifts those bent beneath their loads. The eyes of all look to you in hope; you give them their food as they need it. When you open your hand, you satisfy the hunger and thirst of every living thing. The Lord is righteous in everything he does; he is filled with kindness. The Lord is close to all who call on him, yes, to all who call on him in truth. He grants the desires of those who fear him; he hears their cries for help and rescues them. The Lord protects all those who love him, but he destroys the wicked. I will praise the Lord, and may everyone on earth bless his holy name forever and ever.

ACKNOWLEDGMENTS

I thank God for the precious gift of His Holy Spirit, who revealed the wonderful goodness of God to me through our living Lord Jesus Christ. Praise, honor, and glory be to God for enabling me to write and publish these testimonies and to experience His marvelous goodness in every moment of my life.

A special thanks to those the Lord brought alongside to help in this endeavor; Roland Meloche, George Nottaway, Maria Chapeskie and Monique for your prayers, encouragement, help, and support.

I thank those who answered the call of God to join me in His work and those who came to help in Rapid Lake and Maiganajik; Ben Lafreniere, Maurice and Betty Lesage, Michel and Melissa Bervaldi, Guylaine St. Georges, Debbie Van Horne, Raymond, Peter, Mark, Gary Fontaine, Valerie Whittaker, the Korean Missionaries, Joseph Lafontaine, Pastor Rose, Pastor Gerry and Bridgette Ingravelle, Ron and Mary Draper, Jean-Pierre and Mario.

The 700 Club in Canada for partnering in this work, as well as members of the Northfield Pentecostal Church, the Little Brown Church in Renfrew, Ontario, and Pastor Mark Redner from WCCA in Kinburn, Ontario. The Catholic Women's League (CWL) in Renfrew and Cobden Ontario.

Rose Lepack for the many hours you spent sewing, knitting, and making quilts for the First Nations communities, Darlene Barr, Mabel Proulx, Don, Kenny and Christine, Shirley and Rob Kluke, as well as Phyllis Pitt, who all helped by gathering and donating clothing and household items for the First Nations Mission.

The staff and volunteers of Queen Elizabeth Elementary School, Kazabazua, Quebec, for their generosity in helping the Native School in Rapid Lake.

To those whose names are not mentioned, including my family who prayed, encouraged, and supported this work in your own quiet way, the Lord knows you and He will honor and reward your faithfulness.

Chapter 1

MIRACLES

Psalm 111

*Praise the L*ORD*!*

*I will thank the L*ORD *with all my heart*
  as I meet with his godly people.
*How amazing are the deeds of the L*ORD*!*
  All who delight in him should ponder them.
Everything he does reveals his glory and majesty.
  His righteousness never fails.
He causes us to remember his wonderful works.
  *How gracious and merciful is our L*ORD*!*
He gives food to those who fear him;
  he always remembers his covenant.
He has shown his great power to his people
  by giving them the lands of other nations.
All he does is just and good,
  and all his commandments are trustworthy.
They are forever true,
  to be obeyed faithfully and with integrity.
He has paid a full ransom for his people.
  He has guaranteed his covenant with them forever.
  What a holy, awe-inspiring name he has!
*Fear of the L*ORD *is the foundation of true wisdom.*
  All who obey his commandments will grow in wisdom.
Praise him forever!

Journal Entry - May 2009

One day on my way to clean homes, I was listening to the radio and heard that Michael W. Smith was coming to the Woodvale Pentecostal Church in Ottawa.

The tickets for the concert were thirty-five dollars per person and selling out quickly. Instantly, I knew that I was going. I didn't have the money to buy tickets, but that didn't bother me because I knew that I would go. I didn't need to know how it would happen.

Later that week, I had a new client call to ask if I could clean her home. It was an older home and the shower was covered in rust stains. I didn't want to leave the shower this way and I knew that I couldn't get the rust off without the Lord's help. I told Him, Lord, I can't leave the shower like this, please help me, I want it to be clean, it looks awful.

I found a spray bottle in the kitchen cupboard and I thanked the Lord. It was a yellow spray bottle and it was for kitchen and bath. I don't wear rubber gloves. I scrubbed and prayed and the rust came off. I was so excited because I knew that the client would be thrilled to have her shower look like new again.

Before I got home, my hands were red and hurt very badly. Tiny cuts appeared all over my hands and then I realized that the chemical in the spray bottle had burned my hands very badly. I asked the Lord to heal my hands.

Three days later, on a Saturday morning, two Christian brothers came knocking on my door. They asked if I would like to go with them to a free Christian concert in Pembroke, Ontario. I went with them.

We arrived, and as soon as we found seats to sit down, a man on stage asked if there were any Michael W. Smith fans present and four of us put up our hands, all ladies. He said that he had two concert tickets to give away. As soon as he said that, I blurted out, "Wow, that's how the Lord will do it."

MIRACLES

I instantly knew that the people who brought me there were thinking that I was being very arrogant, but I just knew it.

He continued speaking and said that after the intermission he wanted three ladies to come to the stage. He would explain how one of them could win the tickets. I left the building at intermission with the people that I had arrived with and when we came back into the building after intermission, we all noticed that there were three ladies at the front with this man.

The people who were with me immediately said, "Guess it's too late," but I walked to the front and stood with the three ladies. One of them looked at me and asked if I would like to have Michael W. Smith tickets and I said yes, I would love to. The man looked at me and said, "You are one," and then he looked at the lady who asked me if I would like to have the tickets and told her that she was the other. He looked at the other two and said, "One of you will be the other," then one of them walked away.

We were told to go up on stage and join three children and three men. The children held little paper water cups filled with cotton balls. The men held empty cups. We were given empty cups and instructed to take the cotton balls from the children's cups and put them into the men's cups. The one who finished first would win the tickets. We could not use our hands. We had to dip our noses into a cup filled with Vaseline.

The announcer held the cup filled with Vaseline. When he said, "Go," we were to run, but as he was saying this the Lord told me not to run. The Lord said, "Walk." Before I could get the first cotton ball, the lady who asked me if I wanted the tickets had finished and won the tickets.

I was thrilled for her and I rejoiced with her. Then the announcer handed out tissues for us to wipe the Vaseline off our noses. I had already wiped it off with my hands and was rubbing it into my hands as I walked back to my seat.

As I walked and was rubbing the Vaseline into my hands, the Lord healed my hands! My hands were perfectly healed and more beautiful than I ever remembered them to be! They were completely healed before I got back to my seat!

When I realized what was happening I started to shout, and when I got to my seat I showed the people who were with me. They had seen how badly burned my hands were before and now they were amazed to see that the Lord had healed me, and they rejoiced with me. They were also certain that I was not going to go to the Michael W. Smith concert. They were sure that I was wrong about getting the tickets.

When the concert was over, we turned to leave. The lady who had won the tickets came running toward me. She put the tickets in my hand. I said, "Did the Lord tell you to do this?" She said, "Yes, He did," and she was leaping with joy because she had heard the Lord's voice and obeyed Him.

Only God knows the impact this had on those who were with me. Glory be to God, He is absolutely awesome.

Journal Entry – October 2010

What an amazing day. The Lord is so good. This morning I was awakened by the telephone. One of my customers called to cancel the cleaning of her home today and I only had one home to clean. I asked the Lord what He would have me do, and He reminded me that I had asked for time to visit my Mom with my Aunt Elaine, Mom's only sister.

I phoned my aunt and we drove to visit my Mom. We had a wonderful visit and a time of prayer together. The nurse was surprised to see us and said that five minutes before we arrived, she had phoned my sister because my Mom needed slippers. I brought slippers with me for her. Praise God.

When I got home, I was sending an email to George at the 700 Club in Canada. While typing the email, the telephone rang. It was the local car dealer. He had just spoken to George at the 700 Club and said that he had just discussed the van with them, and he told me that George wanted me to email him.

Within minutes, I had an email response back informing me that by using my car as a trade-in, the van would be purchased by the 700 Club for my ministry. Praise God! What wonderful news!

A few minutes after receiving this news, the Lord prompted me to go to my garage. I didn't know why, but when I opened the garage door I noticed a Tim Horton's coffee, sitting on a shelf, still warm, and just the way I like it. I thanked the Lord for it and noticed a bright, red vest sitting on top of four bags. I opened one of the bags and could hardly believe what I saw!

Beautiful new clothing and I knew they were for me. They were my size. This was much needed and beyond what I would have ever even thought of asking the Lord for. How great is our Father that He should care so wonderfully for our every need.

I don't know who brought them, but I do know who sent them. I was so awestruck that I could hardly speak, but had to tell someone. I phoned Monique and shared the news. She is a precious sister and my prayer partner. She had phoned me earlier to tell me that the Lord said He was sending things for me. We rejoiced together and she shared how the Lord moved in her life today also. We are so blessed to be children of God.

This evening Mabel, a lady from the Catholic Women's League, invited me out for coffee at the local Tim Horton's. I shared with her what the Lord was doing and we rejoiced together in the Lord.

When I got home, I had a message on my answering machine. It was from my Aunt Elaine, telling me that she wants to give me four snow tires, rims included, for the van.

She said she was doing this as a contribution to the ministry to spread the Gospel. Glory be to God!

I am reminded of the word, *"Seek first the Kingdom of God and His righteousness and all of these things shall be added unto you."* His Kingdom is living a life of goodness, peace, and joy in the Holy Spirit. His righteousness is in Him and we are in Him. We must remain "in Him" because everything is in Him. Glory be to God. The fullness of God is in Christ. We are complete in Him.

Hospital Emergency Room – October 2012

Last week, I spent an entire morning witnessing to patients and staff in the local hospital Emergency Room.

My daughter phoned me to tell me that she had a dream. My daughter is a nurse. She was concerned about me and said that in the dream she was with me in the Emergency Room of a hospital. Something had happened, I was being seen by the Triage Team, and they were not taking my condition seriously.

In the dream, she told them that I was a Christian with a lot of faith in God. She said if I was there, it was serious. They were not paying attention and were not alarmed as she was.

She saw that when I opened my mouth, blood came gushing out. She woke up alarmed and phoned to tell me. I told her that I would go to the hospital just to get a good report and call her back to ease her mind.

I drove to the hospital and spent the entire time witnessing to everyone I met. Glory be to God. It's amazing how many of them were believers. These precious hospital workers need encouragement. We were all blessed.

One of the nurses shared a story with me. She told a story of a little girl who was dying in the hospital. The little girl opened her eyes and told the nurse, "I have to go now, the angels are here and they are so beautiful, I have to go with them now." Then the child left. This nurse told me that she will never forget what this child said before she left. Praise God.

The results of the tests they performed on me were perfectly normal and I gave the good news to my daughter. Praise be to God. I am constantly amazed at how the Lord changes everything. He is among us. Praise His holy name.

Vacuum Cleaner – January 2013

Last week, I cleaned my employer's home as a favor to him. He was not there. As I was about to leave, I felt the Lord prompt me to take his vacuum cleaner. I was reluctant to do it, but felt very strongly that the Lord wanted me to take it. So I did.

Driving away, with his vacuum cleaner on the back seat, I said, "Lord, what am I doing with the vacuum cleaner?" He said, very clearly, "You are going to fix it." I thought, "Good Lord, I don't know how to fix vacuum cleaners!"

I knew that I would have to call my employer and tell him that I had his vacuum cleaner. I was worried about what he would think, so I asked the Lord to tell me what to say to him and the Lord said, "Tell him you are going to fix it." As soon as I got home I phoned my employer and told him. He asked, "Do you fix vacuum cleaners?" I said, "No." I felt very foolish, but told him that I would try. I hung up the phone and then I phoned Sears to ask them if they could tell me how to fix a vacuum. They told me that I would need to look in the manual. I didn't have the manual. I only had the vacuum.

A little later, as I was sitting down, I asked the Lord to help me. I didn't know what to do and I asked Him to show me what to do. I turned the vacuum over and noticed a number 40110. I looked up and noticed a little red, plastic toolbox sitting on a shelf. My eyes seemed to be fixed on this little red box. I said, "Lord, is there something in that box that I need?"

I walked over to the shelf, picked up the little red box, and opened it. I lifted out a little tray inside the box and noticed a clear plastic bag with SEARS written on it. I thought, "Oh, Lord, is this for the vacuum?" Then I noticed a number written on the bag, 40110. I got so excited because I knew that this was the same number I had seen under the vacuum. The Lord showed me exactly how to install the part and the vacuum was fixed.

I brought the repaired vacuum to the office. When my employer arrived, I showed him that it worked and I told him, exactly the way I am telling you, how the Lord had orchestrated this.

He was amazed and told me that the vacuum was given to him by his mother and it had never worked. He also told me that he had tried to find someone to fix it, but could not.

I have been talking to my employer about the Lord Jesus for two years. This miracle confirmed what I've been telling him: Jesus is alive and he is Lord. The Lord knows everyone and everything. He knows how to reach people with His loving kindness. Glory be to God.

Two Silver Coins - 1999

Results from a series of medical tests came back with a diagnosis of cancer, but I did not believe it for a second. The tests were performed three times, and each time they came back with the same report: *cancer*. I still did not believe it for a moment.

My family was very distraught and upset with me for not believing the diagnosis. My doctor informed me that I would have to go for treatment and surgery to have the cancer removed. Although I didn't believe the diagnosis, I agreed to go.

As my sister drove to the appointment with the oncologist, my daughter was sitting in the back seat. I sat in the front passenger seat. I remember turning and saying to my sister, "This is a waste of time, it's a mistake and there is no cancer." She and my daughter both burst into tears and I felt so badly for them. I had no idea that these words were going to come out of my mouth because I wasn't even thinking about this. I knew they were thinking that I was "in denial," but I honestly did not believe that there was the slightest possibility of cancer. I was totally convinced. We drove the rest of the way in complete silence and I had such a marvelous peace in my heart.

In the waiting room there were many sad people waiting to be called in for their treatments, and then it was my turn. I will never forget the look on the doctor's face when he saw me. He looked at me, then looked at the file, and with an odd look on his face he shook his head and said, "I have never seen this before but there has been a mistake. There is no cancer, but to be certain we will do another test." Praise be to God, *there was no cancer*. I came out of that room leaping and filled with the joy of the Lord shouting, *"There is no cancer!"* By the look on their faces, I don't think my daughter and sister believed me.

We left the hospital and walked toward the vehicle. My sister got to the car first. My daughter was walking beside me and we heard my sister shout, *"Oh my God, look at this!"* My spirit leapt within me because I knew the Lord had done something. She was pointing to the door handle. The door handle on the car was not more than a half inch wide and there sitting on it, *"against the law of gravity,"* were two mint condition 1969 silver dollar coins.

I knew in my heart that this was confirmation from the Lord that He had just performed a miracle and they certainly could not explain this one away. Then suddenly I remembered the story Jesus told of *the Good Samaritan* and *"two silver coins"* recorded in the Book of Luke. The Lord takes care of me. Praise His holy name forever.

Cardiac Miracle – November 11, 2011

I called the 700 Club while having a heart attack and received prayer. Debbie, a Christian sister who lives with me, called 911 and I was taken to the local hospital. Accompanied by a doctor and a nurse, I was transferred to the Heart Institute in Ottawa.

On Sunday, November 13th, I was released from the hospital. The cardiologist told me that the procedure they performed to unblock the artery was "excellent and the timing of the entire episode was perfect."

The right place at the right time, with all the right people in place from start to finish. I was back at work on Tuesday the 15th. Praise, honor, and glory be to God, and thank you to the 700 Club for being there. The first step is prayer. Then the result came, a miracle from the hand of our heavenly Father through Christ Jesus, our wonderful Lord.

On the 21st of January 2012, my cardiologist told me there was no need for another follow-up visit. The results of the tests were perfectly normal. Praise God.

Where to Find Water

A young couple were building a home and trying to do it debt-free. They had become quite discouraged because they could not find water. I prayed with them, on the telephone, asking the Lord to help them. The Lord showed me where the water was. I told them they would find it "under the machine in the front of the house to the right."

Within weeks, I received news from them that there was a machine parked in front of their home and the water was found in the exact place the Lord had showed me. Praise be to God, He is so Good!

The Onion

One evening, a Christian brother, Roland, came to stay overnight in my home. I knew he must be hungry and started looking for something to feed him. I had bread and a can of tuna and mayonnaise, but no onions.

I started to prepare the sandwiches while Roland was sitting at the table. He had seen me open the fridge twice and he knew that I had looked for onions but there were none. He was sitting in a position where he could clearly see the empty crisper when I opened the fridge. I opened the fridge for the third time, and to our amazement there was a beautiful big fresh onion, sitting right where we could both see it.

As we were rejoicing and thanking the Lord for providing the onion, the phone rang. It was Michel, calling to ask if he could stay overnight also. He said the Lord told him to phone me. I told him about the onion and he said that he had a dream the night before and in the dream someone was giving him a sandwich!

The Lord cares about the smallest details of our lives. What an awesome, loving Lord we serve.

Spiritual Warfare and Gold Dust – August 2012

This testimony was received from a co-worker who wanted to attend a Wednesday evening 'healing room' at my home. She told me that she felt a sudden oppression, and rather than come to my home, she came to our office. She didn't know what to do and the oppression was getting worse. Suddenly, she remembered what she had heard me say when I had prayed for her husband. She repeated what she remembered me saying. She said, "I rebuke you in the name of the Lord Jesus Christ."

She said that suddenly a warm feeling came over her and she felt tingling all over her body and the oppression suddenly left. Praise be to God. While she was sharing this testimony with me at work, gold dust started to appear on my hands. It seemed to be coming right out of my pores. I remembered hearing about the appearance of gold dust before, but it had never happened to me. Glory be to God.

I am in awe of the goodness of God and the power in the name of Christ Jesus our Lord and the work of the Holy Spirit. Glory be to God.

Power of Prayer – Family Restoration – Christmas 2012

This Christmas, thanks be to God, will be spent with my daughter, son-in-law, and my three precious grandchildren. This will be our first Christmas together in eight years.

In answer to prayer, the Lord restored my family after eight years of being without my daughter and three grandchildren. In a moment's time, the Lord restored us as a family. Glory be to our wonderful, loving Father and Christ Jesus our Lord.

The Holy Spirit moved so quickly, it's difficult to remember what happened. My daughter put my newest granddaughter in my arms, introduced me to the second and the precious eldest one. I remember saying, "I love you," to my daughter, and she said, "I know."

Shortly before this happened, I remembered thinking, *"There is power in prayer,"* and instantly the Lord said, "You're about to see how much." I was awake until 5:00am one morning, praying for my family, actually *"crying in tongues,"* and the next day I received this wonderful miracle of family restoration. Glory be to God. I am in awe of the loving kindness of our Heavenly Father. His love overwhelms me!

If you are praying for loved ones, don't give up. Keep praying. There is power in prayer. God is faithful.

Light Bulbs – December 2012

Two weeks ago, the lamp in my living room started to flicker and then went out. It's unusual to have to replace light bulbs in my home, and I was not sure if I had any to replace it with. As I was wondering whether I had any, "suddenly" a dark pink gift bag flashed in my mind and I knew instantly where this bag was. I opened the linen closet and sure enough, there was the gift bag. I thought, now this would be an odd place to find a light bulb. I looked in the bag and noticed a package of four odd light bulbs and wondered what they were doing there. They certainly didn't fit the lamp and I didn't know why I would even have bulbs like that. Then, I put the bag back and took a bulb from a lamp that I was not using and replaced the burned out one.

The following week, Roland came by and offered to bring furniture to my daughter for me, and I also brought them two lamps that had been given to me. One of them didn't have a switch and I wanted to be certain that it worked. So I took off the shade and noticed that the bulb was burned out. I said, "Oh my good Lord, can it be?" Roland looked at me a little oddly, wondering what had happened, but I didn't say anything. I wanted to be sure. I went to the linen closet and got the package of four odd bulbs. I opened it, and sure enough, they fit the lamp perfectly.

Then I told Roland how I had seen the bulbs the week before and I was praising God for this blessing. Then the Lord said, "Look at the price on the package." I looked and I saw 3.17. I showed this to Roland and told him that my daughter's birthday is March 17. Glory be to God.

Roland went to the hardware store and found a switch. They only had one, and he fixed the lamp.

When I shared this with my daughter and son-in-law, they were amazed too, especially when they saw the 3.17, my daughter's birth date! I have been witnessing to them also and the Lord is confirming His Word with some unusual miracles. These miracles get the attention of those to whom we witness, and their hearts are open to receive the wonderful goodness of God through Christ Jesus, our Lord.

Safety Pins – December 2012

The Lord has been doing some "unusual miracles." On the 13th of December, I drove to Beloeil, Quebec, with my aunt, and we stopped at a restaurant on our way. I went into the "ladies room" and noticed two "new" safety pins sitting on the top of the toilet paper dispenser. As soon as I saw them, the Lord said, "Put them in your pocket." I was embarrassed but felt very strongly that I should do it. Reluctantly, I picked them up and as I was putting them in the pocket of the "white sweater" that I was wearing, one of the safety pins fell to the floor and under the adjacent stall. I didn't pick it up. The other was in my pocket.

Ten days later, as I was getting ready to go and spend Christmas with my daughter and her family, the Lord told me to wear my white sweater. It was on the sofa, and just before going out the door, I put it on.

While I was at my daughter's home, I gave them some things that the Lord had prompted me to bring. They were amazed at the items because they had a conversation before I arrived about needing the very things that I brought. This was confirming to them what I had told them about the Lord, that He knows everything and nothing is hidden from His sight and that He is our provider.

I went downstairs and my granddaughter was upstairs. I heard her ask, "Does anyone have a couple of safety pins?" Instantly, I realized that the sweater I was wearing was the same one that I had on when the Lord told me to pick up the two safety pins and I blurted out, "Oh My Lord!" My granddaughter heard me and came running down the stairs. At the same time, I reached into my pocket to retrieve the safety pin. She said, "Oh Nan! Don't tell me that you have two safety pins!"

I felt terrible because I remembered that I had not picked up the one that had fallen on the floor. I took the one safety pin out of my pocket and told her how the Lord had told me to put both in my pocket. It was obvious that He knew that she would need them. I told her how one had fallen on the floor and I had not picked it up. While I was telling her this, my hand was still feeling around inside my pocket. Suddenly, I felt another safety pin, and she noticed the surprised look on my face. I gave it to her, saying, "I did not put it there. The Lord did this." It's amazing how the Lord will use foolish things to confound us, and at the same time, demonstrate His wonderful goodness. Praise His Holy Name.

Miracle Debt Cancellation (written by Debbie) – March 2012

Lorraine and I (Debbie) prayed, asking the Lord to help me pay off my credit card debts. I called the most overdue one first. I reached a voice mailbox and left a message for the person to return my call. I called the next one and they told me that my account had been sent to collections and they gave me another phone number to call. I called and gave all the information they requested, including my social insurance number. They couldn't find anything. I realized then that the Lord had paid off my debt of approximately $8,000.

One day, my daughter called to let me know that mail was delivered to her house for me. There was an application to apply for a credit card. It was the same company I had the debt with. I thought, "If I still owed money to them, I am sure they wouldn't want me to have another credit card." I believe God did this to confirm to me that this debt is paid, just as Jesus paid for my sins. Isn't the Lord amazing? I have heard about this happening to other people, but never thought it would happen to me. My Lord loves me and has shown me His love in many ways. This is one of His glorious miracles in my life. Praise be to God. My Father loves me, I am His daughter, and I truly love Him.

Provision – September 2012
Yesterday, before going to work, I looked in the freezer to find something to feed our growing family. There are nine of us now. I found a package of ten chicken drumsticks and then thought, *Lord, this is not much to feed four adults, two teenagers, two elementary students and a two-year-old, but I hope that it will do.*

Moments later, I received a phone call from Rose, a precious lady who knits and sews clothing for me to bring on missions. She called to say, "I heard that you have brought a new family from Maiganajik to live with you and thought that you may need some extra food. Would you be able to use two big chickens?" Praise God! I told her that I had just been talking to the Lord about that very thing. Rose asked me to come over to her house right away and get them.

While I was away, the two-year-old broke a cup. This particular cup had just been given to me. I arrived to pick up the chickens and Rose also gave me a bag with three new cups in it. The Lord is so good.

(Mabel - 2nd row on left)

The Goodness of God – Summer 2011

What a tremendous blessing to meet this family. Late one evening, the Lord prompted me to go to the local grocery store. I didn't need anything, but I obeyed the Lord and went.

As I entered the store, I noticed a man with several children. I stopped and counted them. It was unusual to see a man with this many children. I counted several and then asked the man if these were his children. He didn't speak English, so I asked him in French and he said, "Yes."

He told me that he had ten children and just then his wife arrived with two little ones. They told me their eldest child had stayed at home. They arrived in two vehicles.

I realized at once that I had clothing for this family. I had tried to give away the clothing that came to mind, but somehow could not. I knew it was for them, so I told him that I had clothing for his family. He seemed a little surprised and asked, "How much?" I said, "Nothing."

I explained to him how the Lord used me to give clothing and food to people, and how I just knew that there was clothing that had come in especially for them.

He seemed a little uneasy, but I assured him that I was being honest and did not expect anything in return. I asked the cashier for a pen and paper and I wrote my name, address, and phone number, and told him to come and get the clothing for his family, then I left.

They came to my home the following week and we were all so blessed to see that the Lord had given me everything they needed. To hear them praise the Lord for His goodness when they received food, clothing, toys, and household items, filled my heart with unspeakable joy. I am amazed at the goodness of God. What an awesome God we serve.

They came back this week and I see the light of the Lord in them and His joy filling their hearts. The goodness of God is overwhelming, too great to express in words. His amazing love is beyond my capacity to put into mere words. To witness the transformation in the hearts of those He touches with His love is awesome. Glory be to God.

Amazing Love

Recently, I met a young mother who was in desperate need. Her husband died in her home, she had a nervous breakdown, and her children were taken from her by the Children's Aid Society. She turned to drinking and drugs.

Mabel told me about this young woman and suggested that I could help her. I told Mabel that nothing is impossible with God and I knew He could help her, and I told Mabel to give this girl my phone number.

One night, Mabel phoned and asked me to have coffee with her at a local coffee shop. It was late and I was in bed, but I got dressed, picked Mabel up at her home, and we went for coffee.

A young woman came in and walked up behind Mabel and put her hands over Mabel's eyes. She wanted to surprise her and she was laughing because Mabel didn't know who she was. Then she stood beside us and Mabel asked her if she had called the woman yet. I realized that this was the lady Mabel had talked to me about.

She said she had called but was unable to reach the lady. I looked at her and said, "Honey, I am the woman."

I got up and hugged her and said "something"—to be honest, I don't know what I said to her. She seemed to instantly change, her whole countenance changed. I don't know what the Lord did or how He did it, but from the moment I met her she stopped drinking, stopped taking drugs, and she is full of His peace, all the time. It's amazing to witness the change the Lord makes in a person. I am in awe of the goodness and mercy of our Lord.

The Lord put it on my heart to clean her home and accompany her to court appearances, lawyer appointments, and meetings with the Children's Aid Office. She will have her children home for Christmas. I met Susan in October.

She now has her children two days a week. She has been attending a local church on a regular basis, and is also hosting Bible study groups in her home on a weekly basis. Glory be to God, Susan is just one of the many whose lives have been transformed by our wonderful Lord Jesus Christ.

With God, all things are possible.

I witness this truth on a daily basis. There are days when I could write volumes on what the Lord is doing. What an awesome God we serve. The more I know Him, the more I want to know Him, and the less I can express how awesome He is with mere words. He is so much greater than words. In Him we live and move and have our being. He is everything. Glory be to God.

MIRACLES

I can't express the awesome joy and wonder I experience when the love of God touches and changes a life. The only word that comes to mind is *awe*.

Chapter 2

HEALINGS

No More Wheelchair, Cane or Scooter – August 28, 2012

At 4:55 this afternoon, I was about to lock up the model homes and close the office for the day, but suddenly I knew that I had to wait. I had an appointment to get the oil changed in my vehicle after work and it was later than usual for me to close up the model homes, but I waited. At 4:57, a vehicle pulled up in front of the office and a gentleman came in with his wife.

They stopped just inside the door and I told them that they had arrived just in time. I noticed that the lady was crippled and she was in pain. Her husband helped her into my office and I asked him what was wrong with his wife. She answered and said that she had rheumatoid arthritis and that they needed to get a home that was wheelchair accessible. She also had a scooter and would need to have a home that was built to suit their needs. She told me that she couldn't get around in their home anymore, and she was very sad that they would have to leave their home.

They started to describe their preferences for a home, but I knew that the Lord had a different plan for them. I told them to forget about buying a home. I leaned forward on my desk, looked into her eyes, and gave her my testimony of how the Lord had healed me after more than forty doctors had told me that there was nothing they could do for me. I told her how they had not expected me to live very long. I told her how the suffering that I endured for more than three years had taken my hope away and how I just wanted to die.

She started to cry and said, "I want to die too." I told her how a precious woman of faith had prayed for me and I was totally healed. I told her how the Lord healed me and that my faith had soared. I knew that nothing was impossible with God. I told her that I had faith enough to pray for people who were dead and saw the Lord raise them to life. Then I said, "You are not dead and I know the Lord wants to set you free from this infirmity."

I asked her if I could pray for her. She said yes, and she was sobbing. Her husband told me that she had had thirty operations and that she was not able to open her hands. But he recognized that this was a divine appointment set up by God for his wife's healing. I prayed, and the Kingdom of God filled the room, her, her husband, and me, all at the same time.

When I told her that the Kingdom of God had come, she stopped crying, but tears were streaming down her face. Her eyes lit up and then I told her to stretch out her hands and move them. She moved them easily and freely, but I noticed that her thumb was not moving. There was a long scar, from a recent surgery, just below her thumb. I told her to move her thumb and said, "The Lord Jesus heals you." She moved it immediately.

I took her by the hand and she stood to her feet. She was a little shaky, but I said, "Forget about your body and stand up." She stood tall. Then I told her to lift her legs. She lifted her legs. I let go of her hand and she kept lifting her legs freely. Her husband said, "It has been years since I saw her do that."

I told her that soon she would be leaping. Her husband said, "You just missed a sale," but I told him that there was nothing on this planet worth more than watching the Lord Jesus set a person free.

They were ready to leave and I knew they were going to ask my name. I told them, "There is no need for you to know my name. Jesus healed you, it doesn't matter who I am." She left my office, unaided by human means. She walked, with a skip in her step, in front of her husband and down the stairs. I watched from the window of my office as she hopped up into their truck before her husband could get to her to help.

They told me they were from Sudbury, Ontario, and heading to Ottawa. Glory be to God. I am constantly in awe of His amazing love. Nothing is impossible with God!

Healing Miracle – June 8, 2012

Last night, my daughter and grandchildren came to visit and stay overnight. When my eldest granddaughter got out of the vehicle, I noticed that her right leg was bandaged. It looked like she had a cast on her ankle and foot and her knee was bandaged. She told me that she had sprained her ankle and torn ligaments in her knee.

My daughter is a nurse and confirmed the injury. I was sitting on the porch a little later and my granddaughter came and sat beside me. Her leg, all the way down to her toes, was swollen and discolored. I asked her if it was painful and she said "Yes." Then I told her to put the foot on my knee. She did and I asked if it hurt and she said no. Then I told her, when she was an infant and had any type of pain or illness, I would tell her to ask Jesus to take it away, and He always did.

I told her to close her eyes and think about the Lord Jesus, and I would pray. After prayer, while my hands were still on her foot, I asked her if she felt anything and she said she felt heat in the ankle and behind the knee. I told her that the Lord was healing her, and took my hands off of her foot. She put her foot on the ground and stomped it. Without saying anything, she ripped the brace or bandage off of her foot and started wiggling her ankle from side to side. I asked her how it felt and she said, "Great." Then, she looked at the bandage on her knee. I knew that she was wondering if she should take it off. She asked me if she should. I told her that it was common and to go ahead if she wanted to. She did. By the time she got it off, the swelling had gone and the color had returned to normal. She stood up and had no discomfort. She began to walk around.

My daughter came out and I told her that the Lord had just healed her daughter, and I pointed to my granddaughter. My daughter and granddaughter both knew this was a miracle. I told them because they are believers, they can do the same. We lay our hands on the sick and they are healed. The word of God tells us in Mark Chapter 16 that this is one of the signs that follow believers. Glory be to God. We are so blessed to be children of God.

Hospital Visit – August 2012

Recently, Roland and Dorothy came with me to a hospital to pray for the sick. Prior to going, I asked the Lord to go before us and prepare the way. To remove any hindrances, so we could pray without anyone objecting to our being there.

When we got into the elevator, we prayed in tongues, and when we got off the elevator on the second floor, the nurse who was there looked at me and said, "Oh my God, I just told your mother that she would see you today. I just told her, and here you are." We prayed for my Mom and others who were there without any objection or interruption.

I saw a young mother with two children. The young mother recognized me and I asked her how she was. She pointed to one of her children. This child had open sores on her face. I asked the mom if we could pray for her daughter. She said yes, and we did. We laid hands on the child, in the waiting room of the emergency department, and we saw the healing take place. Glory be to God. The Lord is so GOOD.

Healing Testimonies – October 2010

The Lord is moving in a wonderful way. October 28th, 2010, the Lord led me to the hospital in Renfrew to pray for three precious ladies. One of them, Vi Schroeder, gave a wonderful testimony of how the Lord appeared to her from out of a cloud of lightning. He told her that when it was time for her to leave this earth, He would come to take her home. What a precious woman of God. They seemed to know that I was coming to pray for them and they seemed to be expecting me.

On Friday, January 21, 2011, the Lord brought Vi Schroeder home to be with Him. I thank God for Vi's amazing testimony and for her sharing it with us. I have given and shown her testimony to many, and the results are the same. Each time, the presence of God manifests and people are touched by the Lord as they watch and listen.

Glory be to God for leading me to her and capturing her testimony on video before she left. Meeting Vi was one of the greatest blessings I have ever received from the Lord. Her faith in God and our precious Lord Jesus touched me deeply. I thank God for this precious sister in Christ, and I know that we will meet again when the Lord brings me home.

Last week, the Lord led me to a local coffee shop. When I arrived, one of the clerks at the counter had just been burned by hot tea. I took her hand in mine and rebuked the pain and it left instantly. Glory to God.

On Sunday, during a telethon here in Renfrew for the Friends of the Handicapped, a gentleman was telling someone that he was in terrible pain. This man said that he had a severe migraine headache. I laid hands on him and rebuked the pain in Jesus' name, and it left him instantly. Praise God.

Car Accident—May 18, 1994

While driving to a local convenience store one evening, I was involved in a serious car accident. The injuries sustained in the accident affected my spine and left me without the use of my left arm. During the following three years, I saw more than forty-one doctors. There was nothing they could do. I suffered with constant, severe pain. Surgery was finally being scheduled to sever a nerve. The surgeon hoped this procedure would reduce the pain. But the Lord had a better plan for me.

One afternoon, in the summer of 1997, I received a phone call from a neighbor. She had scheduled an appointment with a Christian woman who was to pray for me to be healed. When this woman of God prayed for me, I fell down under the power of God and came up perfectly healed and whole. Praise be to God. The Word of God tells us that "the prayer of faith shall heal the sick," and I am living proof. She prayed in the name of Jesus and I was healed. Praise His holy name forever.

Healing and Salvation – Summer 2011

Darlene Barr and Mabel Proulx arrived with clothing for the First Nations Mission. I invited them to have lunch with me. Darlene mentioned that she was in pain; she had arthritis. When I asked if she was a Christian, she told me that she was a born again Christian. Then why put up with sickness, I asked. She told me that she had been praying and asking the Lord for healing. I asked if I could pray for her, and she agreed. After praying, she told me that during prayer she felt the power of God go through her from head to toe, and said that she almost fell down. Darlene had to leave for an appointment and Mabel wanted to stay longer, so Darlene agreed to come back after the meeting.

Mabel asked if I would give her a copy of a video I had recorded with a testimony from Vi Schroeder and some video footage from Maiganajik. When the video copies were ready, I suggested that we watch them together. As we were watching, Darlene returned with her granddaughter. I invited them to watch the video with us. Darlene recognized Vi Schroeder and said so. She knew Vi, but had lost track of her many years ago.

Her granddaughter thought that this was a coincidence. I told her that there are no coincidences with God. She was here for a reason and the Lord had planned it. I asked her if she was a Christian. She hesitated before saying yes. I asked her if she had received Jesus and she said, "No." I asked her if she wanted to receive Jesus as Savior and Lord and she said, "Yes."

After sharing the message of salvation with her, I asked her if she believed it and she said, "Yes." I prayed for her and then she prayed, asking Jesus to come into her heart and be her Lord and Savior. I gave her one of the booklets that the Lord had me write, to help her understand what to expect.

I am always in awe to see the change that takes place when a person receives Jesus as Lord. Their faces seem to light up and their eyes glisten as they encounter the presence and person of the Holy Spirit, through Christ. Praise, honor and glory be to God. WOW.

Healing Miracle in Kazabazua, Quebec – Autumn 1998

As I was waking up this morning, the Lord reminded me of a healing miracle that took place in my home one evening, while I was living in Kazabazua, Quebec. It was shortly after supper, and someone came knocking on my door. When I opened the door, I saw a local man and I could see that he was in terrible pain. I asked him what had happened and he told me that he had been at a rodeo and was thrown from a horse and his back was injured, but rather than go to the hospital, he said, "I know that you can help me." I invited him in and I looked at his back.

There was a large, purple-colored muscle protruding out from behind his right shoulder blade. When I placed my hands on it, the color changed and it instantly went back into place, behind the shoulder blade where it was supposed to be. I asked him if the pain was gone and he said, "Yes." I was so amazed that I couldn't say a thing. He left, completely healed, and I marveled at the wonderful goodness of God, the Word of God in action.

In the Book of Mark, Chapter 16, the Lord said that one of the signs that would follow those who believe is that we would be able to place our hands on the sick and they would be healed. As simple as that! What an awe-inspiring God we serve.

Journal Entry – August 2011

There is more than enough clothing coming in, and the excess I bring to a nearby Christian outreach center where it is given to those in need, and I thank God for this. The van that the 700 Club so graciously helped me to buy enables me to do this, and I thank God for their help.

Wednesday evenings, I bring local new believers to Teen Challenge for fellowship, worship, prayer, and Bible studies. The Lord is changing their lives in a wonderful way. What a privilege to see Him transform lives.

Last Wednesday, I went to clean four model homes and the sales person was there in the office. She was having problems with her eyes. She had an infection in her eyes and the medications that she was given by her doctor were not helping. Normally, she wore glasses, but even with her glasses she was having difficulty seeing well enough to drive.

I asked her if I could pray and ask the Lord to heal her, and she agreed. I placed my hands on her eyes and prayed. I could feel the anointing on her eyes while I was praying. I took my hands off and noticed that approximately ten feet away from her, on a window, there was a security decal. It was backwards because it was placed on the outside of the window. I asked her if she could see it, and she said yes. I asked her to tell me the numbers that were on it, and she read three numbers.

Once again, I placed my hands over her eyes and asked her for the second time to read the numbers that she was able to see. She read six of them. I placed my hands over her eyes for the third time and continued to pray for perfect sight.

When I took my hands off of her eyes, I asked her to find something on her desk that she could normally not be able to see without her glasses. She picked up a sales contract and told me that she would usually have to wear her glasses to see what was written on it. I asked her to tell me what she could see, without glasses on. She looked at it and told me that she could see everything written on it clearly.

We praised the Lord together, and she thanked the Lord for healing her and restoring her sight.

No Time or Distance in the Spirit – September 2008

One night, I had a muscle spasm behind my right shoulder blade and I couldn't sleep. At midnight, as I was walking through the living room, suddenly the Holy Spirit told me to turn on my television. I turned it on and there was a program playing called, "The Hour of Healing," with Richard Roberts on the screen.

As soon as I turned on the television, I saw him turn his head and look up, he said, "Okay, Lord, I will tell her." I just knew that the Lord had told him something to say to me. I know this sounds weird, but I just knew it.

He continued speaking with his wife and they read some healing testimonies. The very next one was from someone named Lorraine from Ohio. Although it was not me, it was my name, and as soon as he said it, my spirit leaped within me. I was expecting a word from the Lord for me. I didn't know what it would be, but I knew that a word was coming, just for me, and I could hardly wait to hear it.

After they had finished reading some testimonies, he said, "Earlier the Lord gave me a word for someone watching. You have a knot in the muscle just behind your right shoulder and the Lord is healing you."

As he spoke, he was moving his hand, and I felt heat on my back where the spasm was. Instantly the spasm left, and I had no more pain. I was amazed at what had just happened.

I phoned the number on the screen to give my testimony, and found out that this had been a pre-recorded program from a different time zone.

The Lord revealed to me, not only does He heal, and is ever present, but He had planned for me to be watching. This television program was taped long before I watched it.

The Lord created time, but He is not subject to it. What an amazing, awe-inspiring Father we have! It will take eternity to grasp the wonderful goodness of God.

Personal Healing – January 2013

In December 2012, I was diagnosed with emphysema in the right lung. Breathing was difficult, but today at work, the Lord softly spoke to me, saying, "I have come that you may have life."

It thrills my heart and soul when the Lord speaks to me, and I was completely enveloped with His blessed presence in that moment. I realized that my lungs were completely clear and I had absolutely no problem breathing.

The Lord healed me as He spoke. Wonderful Lord Jesus, thank You, thank You, thank You for Your mercy, Your grace and Your loving kindness. And Father, thank You for sending Your word and healing me, through Christ Jesus, our wonderful Savior and Lord. This is the wonderful goodness of God!

Healing of Back – December 2012

A young woman had injured her back and was in a great deal of pain. I laid my hands on her back. I felt something move beneath her skin, under my hands, and I knew that it was the power of God. She felt it and I felt it twice, moving up and down the spine. It happened when I declared that

Jesus took our infirmities in His own body on the cross, and by His wounds we are healed. I commanded healing in the name of Jesus Christ. She was completely amazed as she was instantly and powerfully touched and healed in the name of Jesus. Praise His holy name forever.

Chapter 3

TESTIMONIES

Love Keeps No Record of Wrongs Done to It – July 2007

When I purposed in my heart to live the Word of God, I found out just how wretched I was. Some awful things began to surface in my heart, and only by the power of the Holy Spirit were they removed. One of these was bitterness.

I had some very painful memories every time I thought of a specific individual. I thought that I had forgiven the wrong done to me, but the Lord showed me that I had not forgiven "from the heart." He also showed me that I needed the power of the Holy Spirit to do it.

Every time the memories would come, I would say, "I forgive," and one day as I was driving, I passed by this person's house. Once again, all the painful memories came flooding my mind and I said, "Lord, I have forgiven this person, what do You want me to do? Should I tell them how much they hurt me and that I have forgiven them?" Instantly, the Lord answered me with a question. He said "Is that what I did for you?" When the Lord said this, I responded, "Oh no, Lord, You have removed my sin as far from me as the east is from the west and you remember them no more." At the same time, the Holy Spirit brought this Scripture to my mind: "Love keeps no record of wrongs done to it."

Instantly, I knew what the Lord wanted me to do, and I also knew that in and of myself, I could not. I was serious about living His Word, so I answered, "Father, it's obvious that I have kept a record of the wrong done to me, but I don't know where it is or how to get rid of it. I ask You Lord, by the power of Your Holy Spirit, to go and remove this record of the wrong done to me. I don't want to keep any record of any wrong done to me, and I ask You, Father, to do it in the Name of Jesus." The Lord did it and He did it instantly.

Within a week, this person came to my home with severe back pain. I lay my hands on his back and he was healed. Within two weeks of his back being healed, he returned to my home.

As we sat at my kitchen table, he prayed and received Jesus Christ as his Lord and Savior. Because the Holy Spirit did this work in my heart, I was able to pray in sincere love for this person. The word of God also tells us that when we forgive, the Lord forgives also. Love covers a multitude of sins.

Author's Personal Testimony

My Mom's grandfather was a Baptist minister. I loved listening to my Mom reading Bible stories to me when I was a little girl. I remember praying for her whenever she was ill, and the Lord always answered my prayers. Many times, He answered before I would finish.

I've witnessed more miracles than I could possibly count. Beginning in my childhood, I have seen the Lord heal people and raise the dead. I would pray for anything, and the Lord answered. The Lord is more real to me than anyone or anything, and I don't remember not knowing Him.

When I was nine years old, some evangelists held a meeting in the Town Hall, located directly across the street from our house. I went to their meeting, and although I don't remember much, I do clearly remember hearing one of them say, "If you would like to make Jesus your personal Lord and Savior, then wait until the end of the meeting and come and see me." I got so excited that I could hardly wait for the meeting to be over. Debbie, a friend of mine, waited and came with me. She remembers his face. I don't remember anything other than asking Jesus to be my personal Lord and Savior and being so very excited.

My life changed even more after this. I saw many more miracles, but some really out of the ordinary things started happening. I didn't question any of the experiences that I had, but most people knew that there was something very "different" about me. I had no fear of anything or anyone. I remember walking into a burning building to rescue someone and not having any sense of danger whatsoever. Although the ceiling fell before me in flames, I didn't even smell of smoke. These things became "normal" for me. I just did it.

I remember being at the scene of an accident in the summer of 1971. One of the accident victims was my older brother. The police were preparing to zipper him up in a body bag. No one seemed to notice that I was there. I remember walking to each of the victims.

There were four bodies scattered on the ground. I stood over each of them, one at a time, as if in a trance, and waited until I knew that they would all be okay, including my older brother. It didn't disturb me that the police were going to put him in a body bag because I had the assurance that he would be okay. I just knew that I knew. I left the same way I got there. It seemed that suddenly I was there and then suddenly I was standing on the road a few hundred feet from my house. I turned to see a very tall man with red, curly hair and kind, blue eyes. He put out his hand to take mine and said, "Your Father asked me to make sure that you get home safely." I placed my hand in his hand and he walked with me into my house.

We passed by the babysitter and my siblings, and they didn't seem to notice us. I lay face down on my Mom and Dad's bed and I remember he touched my back and I felt "goose bumps" all over my body. I also had an awesome sense of peace. A little later, I noticed that he wasn't there anymore. I wanted to know who this man was and where he went. I asked the babysitter and she said, "What man?" No one saw him, but I know that he was there.

All of the accident victims are alive and well today. They were teenagers at the time of the accident and today, forty-two years later, they are all married with families of their own. Nothing is impossible with God.

The Lord Jesus Christ is real. He is alive and He is awesome in and through us. God truly fills all things everywhere with Himself. There is so much more that we don't know and have yet to learn and experience in Him. I have experienced His love, His compassion, His unspeakable joy, and His indescribable peace.

One time the Lord brought me "in the Spirit" to see some marvelous things, but most of all to experience His "beyond our imagination love." I pray that all will come to believe in the Lord Jesus Christ and experience the wonderful goodness of God.

You have not truly lived until you live the life that only God can give you, in Christ Jesus.

Dream – Called to Speak God's Word – October 2006

October 7th, 2006, the Lord visited me in a dream. I had been seeking His will on what work He had planned for me to do. In the dream, the Lord told me to "look." I knew that when I looked, I would see what He wanted me to do.

I saw an open Bible on a pulpit before me, and the fear of the Lord gripped my heart. As I looked, I instantly knew what He was showing me to do. I said, "Lord, I am too afraid of saying something that is not from You." As I spoke, the

Lord commanded, "You speak and let Me be responsible for what they hear." As He spoke, revelation entered my heart.

We must depend completely on the Holy Spirit as we speak and as we listen to others speaking. The dream was realized on October 7th, 2007. Exactly one year later, I was invited to speak at the Northfield Pentecostal Church in Gracefield, Quebec. Scripture tells us that the Holy Spirit will "show us things to come." Glory be to God. His Holy Spirit is wonderful.

Reality of the Invisible – Summer 2008

When I realized that the Lord wanted me to minister to children and tell them about Him, I became very afraid, because I know the consequence of leading a child astray. The fear of the Lord gripped my heart. I asked the Lord this question, "Lord, how do I tell children about you? They have heard so many lies. They have been told so many things that are not true. They have been told that there is a Santa Claus and there is not. They have been told that there is an Easter Bunny and there is none. I don't want them to think the same of You." While saying these things to the Lord, He said, "Prove to them that what they don't see is more real than what they do see." As the Lord spoke, I instantly knew what to do.

I can't explain how I knew, but I knew very clearly. This is what the Lord had me say to the children. I related the entire conversation that I had with the Lord to them. It's amazing how they reacted, almost as though they were daring me to prove this to them. So I asked them, "Do you have thoughts?" They just stared at me. Then I asked, "Can you see them?" Again they just stared at me. Then I said, "We all do, we can't see them, but we know they are real because we have them. But do you know where they come from?" As Christians, we have the mind of Christ. Unbelievers do not, but they can by believing the Gospel and accepting Christ Jesus as Lord.

Holy Spirit Teaches on Prosperity – July 2008

It amazes me how the Lord often answers a question with a question. I know the Holy Spirit is our Teacher.

One day, after hearing many different messages about prosperity, sowing, and reaping all mixed together, I became confused. I stood still in the middle of my living room and said, "Lord, I want to know the truth. I am hearing all these different messages about sowing, reaping, and prosperity, what is the truth?" Instantly He responded with this question, "Do you remember the birds?"

I laughed out loud as I suddenly remembered the Word of the Lord. It is written in the Book of Matthew 6:26, "Look at the birds. They don't plant or harvest or store food in barns, for your heavenly Father feeds them. And aren't you far more valuable to him than they are?"

Glory be to God. I love it when the Lord answers this way. This is forever settled in my heart. My God takes care of me. Praise His holy name.

Journal Entry – March 2011

I brought six bags of clothing to a local Christian outreach center before going to work Wednesday, and they were grateful. I thank God for the ability to do this.

Monday evening I went to work cleaning four model homes. Arriving earlier than usual at the office, the director was still there and he was sick. I asked if I could pray for him to be healed, and he said yes. I told him that there is nothing special about me except that I am a believer in the Lord Jesus Christ and that the Word of God says that one of the signs that follow those who believe is that we lay our hands on the sick and they are healed, the Lord confirming His word. I told him to thank the Lord Jesus for his healing when he received it.

I prayed and went about my work. A short time later, he said that he had heard that I was good with computers. This was because of a miracle that had happened in their office involving a computer. Before he left the office, I told him about how the Lord Himself had performed the miracle with the computer there. It had nothing to do with me, other than my asking the Lord to do it.

The director asked if I would work an additional two days in their office, starting the following Monday. I would be working on the computer. I agreed and thanked him. This is the same company that just gave me work in their office as hostess on weekends, which I started last week, praise be to God.

The Lord is amazing. I was so hesitant to take on this additional work, but I now see that the Lord needs His people everywhere. Souls, souls, precious souls, they can be reached through every means available and the Lord provides the opportunities. Praise His holy name.

To be sure, there is so much more to share, but it is late and I work in the morning, so I will say goodnight and give more news another time. May the Lord be with you and keep you in His perfect peace.

Journal Entry – May 2011

Tonight I drove to Gatineau to clean four homes and finished very early. I knew that there must be a reason to finish so early, so I asked the Lord what He would have me do. I felt that He wanted me to pay a visit to a lady I had prayed for in Ottawa a month or so earlier. I said, "Lord, if You want me to go to see her, then I ask You to prepare her heart to receive Your word and remove anything from her that may stop her from receiving You," and I thanked Him that He goes before me.

When I arrived at her house, the lights were all off, but she seemed to be right at the door when I rang the bell. She was in her nightclothes, but invited me in. After listening to her pour out her heart about persistent illness and pain, I heard her say, "and I do that too." I stopped her and asked her what she meant by that. She didn't seem to remember saying it, but I insisted that she did. I wanted to know what she meant. She thought for a moment and then said, "I pray too." I told her that without Christ Jesus, she can't get what she was praying for. I told her that Jesus brings healing. Accepting Him and what He did for her was what she needed.

I gave her one of the booklets, "My Best Friend can be Your Best Friend too." She read it, understood it, and she received the Lord. I prayed with and for her and she received her healing. During the prayer to receive the Lord in her heart, her telephone rang, but we ignored it. After prayer, she was filled with the Holy Spirit and she could feel the manifest presence of the Lord all over her.

I sensed in my spirit that the telephone call that came during prayer was from her mother. I told her to call her mom and tell her that she had just received Christ Jesus into her heart as Lord and Savior. She called, and sure enough, it was her mom who had called.

Her mom was thrilled and told her that she had been in persistent prayer all day for this. Glory to God, the harvest is truly ripe.

Women's Ministry Report to 700 Club Canada – September 2011

I called the 700 Club prayer partners a few weeks ago to pray for the New Ministry to Women, and the results are astounding. The women are here, praise be to God. We are living in our new home provided by our heavenly Father. The women are safe and we have everything we need.

There are so many hurting women in the Body of Christ, and they need safe places to live. We have all received more than enough to care for one another, and when it is used wisely, we are all blessed.

Show Them My Love

The moment the girls arrived, they felt their burdens lift and the presence and peace of our precious Lord and Savior Jesus Christ filled their hearts, Glory be to God. Only He can provide what we truly need, His blessed presence and love. Joy fills our home and hearts.

The Lord gave me favor with the car dealer who sold us the van. The van had some "issues," and I didn't feel secure to travel with it to Hanover to pick up Debbie and bring her home.

The Lord put it on my heart to rent a vehicle. I took the van in for service and asked the car dealer if he would consider renting me a reliable vehicle for the seventeen-hour trip to pick up Debbie. He said yes right away and only charged $50 for the rental of one of his used cars for the trip. Praise be to God.

The Lord gave me the energy and strength to drive to Hanover and bring Debbie home. Debbie received the Lord with me when I was nine years old and she was ten. We haven't seen each other for more than thirty years. What a tremendous blessing to have my precious sister in Christ living here.

The love we share in Christ is beyond anything the world knows. We share the same Spirit of the living God, and the love of our Father in Christ our Lord creates a bond that is truly amazing. We see more miracles and manifestations of the Spirit together in Christ. Glory be to God. We serve an awesome God.

The move to our new home was filled with miracles, signs, and wonders. The movers witnessed these miracles and welcomed the Gospel before the move was over. Praise be to God.

I am so grateful for the 700 Club prayer partners being there to pray and encourage us. May the Lord bless them in their faithful service to the Body of Christ and all the work they do in His name.

The new home has a large garage that is heated and perfect for the distribution of food and clothing that comes in for the poor and needy.

I work seven days and three nights a week, and I am grateful to have the help. The strength the Lord provides is a tremendous testimony to those who "see" what the Lord is doing in and through me. This is a miracle. No human strength could accomplish this.

When asked, "How do you do what you do?" I tell them, "With God all things are possible." I am not alone. God is with me. The strength comes from Him. I work hard so I don't have to depend on others to provide for this ministry. God is faithful to give me the strength. He establishes and blesses the work of my hands. All glory goes to Him.

The work the Lord has given me to do pays the rent and covers our expenses. There is plenty left over to buy food for the communities that we minister to in Northern Quebec. It seems we always have what they need, and for others who come to help. The Lord is good.

Women's Ministry Report to 700 Club Canada – October 2011

I've been receiving calls from young mothers in desperate need here in Renfrew. At the moment, I have a young mother and her child staying here. I found them on the street last week. The little girl, five-and-a-half years old, was singing in tongues here yesterday, glory to God.

The little one gave me half the candies she got from going door to door on Halloween. She said, "God told me to give them to the children that don't have anything." Praise God.

The mother and her child have both received the Lord and it's an awesome sight to see. The Lord is moving in their lives in an amazing way. They know that Christ lives in them. Wow.

It seems that the sowing and harvest are happening together. What an amazing outpouring of the Holy Spirit we are in. The opportunities to declare the Gospel are endless and all around us. The Holy Spirit is drawing people to Christ. Glory be to God! What a time to be alive!

I am preparing another DVD to send to you with an awesome testimony from Vi Schroeder. I met Vi at the local hospital when I went there to pray for the sick. She had a tangible encounter with our risen Lord Jesus and shared her testimony on video. It's a truly amazing testimony that I want to share with all of you. She actually touched the Lord's robe and described the texture of the garment He was wearing. She also saw the holes in His hands and feet from the nails.

May the grace of our Lord Jesus Christ, the love of God and the fellowship of the Holy Spirit be with you.

Thank you so much for your prayers and support. The Lord sees, knows, and is pleased that we are working together in the harvest.

It's amazing to see how Debbie is growing in the Lord. She is a wonderful encouragement to me. She loves the Lord with all of her heart and is being led by the Holy Spirit. I love to see brothers and sisters in Christ growing in the faith as they trust and obey our precious Lord.

Debbie arrived on September 10th and it's amazing to see how the Lord has transformed her in such a short time. What an awesome God we serve. The peace and presence of the Lord is awesome as we keep our home dedicated to the Lord and live His way. We are so blessed.

Hitchhiker – June 2012

Debbie and I just arrived home from cleaning homes in Gatineau. We had an awesome encounter with a hitchhiker. When I stopped to give him a ride, Debbie recognized him as being the same person she saw a couple of weeks earlier on the highway.

When he got in the vehicle, he asked me if I had some water. I had placed a bottle of water on the seat beside him before leaving. I reached into the back seat and handed it to him. I told him that we were Christians and he kept saying that he was certain that he had seen me before. I told him that the Spirit of the Lord was with me and that was why he recognized me.

Suddenly the Lord showed me the building where I was to take him. I told him that the Lord had just shown me where he was to go. He said yes, that he had to be there by 9:30pm.

I typed the name, Shepherds of Good Hope, into the GPS and it came up "in red letters." I have never seen red letters on my GPS before. By this time, the presence of God was so strong in the vehicle that Debbie began to cry.

When we arrived at the destination, I pulled the vehicle over in front of the building and let him out. Just as he was getting out of the vehicle, I heard him say, "Where was the Lord when I was eight years old?" The Lord gave me a word for him and I got out and went around the vehicle to where he was standing and delivered it to him. He walked away and I got back into the vehicle.

Another man, who had been sitting on the sidewalk, came over to the passenger side of the vehicle. The window was open and he peeked in. I told him that we were Christian women and he said he was not a believer. I told him that Jesus loved him and he said, "I don't believe that." Then I asked him his name and he said Jason. I told him to look at me and when he did, I told him that one day he would meet the Lord Jesus and he would know that what I said was true. He backed away and we pulled back onto the street. We could hear him shouting to the people on the sidewalk, "Jesus loves me! Yes, me, Jesus loves me! That woman right there in that vehicle just told me that Jesus loves me!"

We continued driving toward Gatineau. As we approached St. Joseph Boulevard in Hull, Debbie looked at me and said,

"We are in Hull we were just in Ottawa, how...?" Then the joy of the Lord filled her and she started laughing. She couldn't understand how we could have been in Ottawa one moment and then the next moment we were in Hull. Praise be to God. This was her first experience in the timelessness of the glory. Praise God, the Lord is awesome!

Angelic Intervention – July 8, 2012

The love of God is amazing. Early Sunday morning, July 8, 2012, the phone rang and it was a Christian brother the Lord had me phone and pray for the night before. He asked if he could come and spend some time here, for rest in the presence of the Lord. What a blessing to have fellowship with a Christian brother. I left for work and spent the entire time worshipping the Lord and ministering to a Christian sister, my co-worker.

The Lord has blessed us with a place to work where we can enjoy His presence and worship "all the time." The office usually closes at 4:00 pm on Sunday, but I stayed late because I had to prepare our schedule. My co-worker left at closing time and locked up the model homes (we sell homes). I was praying and asking the Lord to help me with the schedule. I needed time off to go to Rapid Lake and Maiganajik, and was not sure how to schedule the time off.

As I sat at the computer, I didn't know what to do. Then suddenly I turned and a man (I thought this was a man) was standing in the doorway of my office. I remember that he looked very excited, but I didn't hear him come in and I don't remember anything that he said. I didn't even stand up to greet him, as I normally would have done. It seemed he was only there for a moment and he left. I suddenly knew how to prepare the schedule, but I didn't put any thought into it. I printed it out and put it in an envelope to bring to my head office.

On my way to clean the model homes for my company, I met "Jeff." These homes are in Kanata and Gatineau, and one of them is used as our head office. I put the envelope on my boss's desk with the schedule inside.

My director called me regarding the schedule. He was questioning the time off that I had scheduled, but before he finished his question, he stopped and somehow I knew that the Lord was speaking to him. Then he said, "It's okay, I know what to do." My co-worker was sitting in front of me at my desk and I told her that he had called about the schedule and that it was okay. Then I took out the schedule and looked at it. I told her how I had prayed about it and that I didn't know how to do it.

Then she mentioned that when she left on Sunday there was a vehicle parked outside our office, but there was no one in it and it had no license plate on it. The model homes were locked up and she remembered thinking that it was odd that there was no one there. I told her about the man who seemed to just appear in the office and how the schedule was done so quickly, and I didn't remember him saying anything, but how I seemed to just know how to do the scheduling.

Only God knows for sure, but we both believe that this was an encounter with an angel sent by the Lord to help because of the prayer for help. The result was that I now have the time off that I need to be in Rapid Lake and Maiganajik with the 700 Club Team. Many more miracles happened the same day, and I will write in another post. Glory be to our great God.

Homeless Man in Ottawa – July 2012

The love of God is amazing. One Sunday evening, July 8th, 2012, I left early to clean homes in Kanata and Gatineau. Suddenly the Lord prompted me to open my wallet and get ready to give a "specific amount of money to someone," as well as two booklets. One of the booklets was the one the Lord had me write in 2009 entitled, "My Best Friend Can Be Your Best Friend Too." Just as I had everything ready and in hand, I was on the exit ramp and noticed a man with a paper cup receiving money from the vehicle in front of me.

I had seen him before in the same place. I put my hand out the window of my vehicle to get his attention. The light was red and he noticed me. He approached my vehicle and as soon as he saw what was in my hand, he started to cry. I told him the Lord loved him and it was the Lord who told me to give it to him because the Lord loves him. His head fell on my shoulder and he was sobbing. Then he said, "My name is Jeff and maybe some time you could talk to me."

The light turned green and as I pulled away, I saw Jeff run up the embankment and he sat down. With his head bowed low on his knees, he was sobbing. I shouted to him, telling him that I was going to park my vehicle and come back to talk to him. I pulled in to the first street and parked behind a large stone building. As I pulled into the parking space, I looked up and noticed a sign: "Reserved for Christian Counselors." I got out of my vehicle, not paying attention to what building this was, and I walked down the street to find Jeff.

When I reached Parkdale Avenue, I noticed someone walking toward me and I waved my arm. It was Jeff, and he waved at the same time and came running to meet me. He said maybe we could find a place to sit and talk. I turned and walked to the building where my vehicle was parked. We sat on the steps in front of the building, and I noticed this was a church, Parkdale Baptist Church. I thought of my great-grandfather, he was a Baptist minister.

We sat down and Jeff told me that he had just gotten out of jail. He had the booklet that I had given him the first time we met and he had a Bible and he read these while he was in jail. I was so blessed to hear him speak of the Lord. I think I was more blessed than he was to hear him speak with such a clear mind, and so solid in the truth of God's Word and knowledge of the Lord.

He asked me to pray for him. I asked him what he would ask the Lord for if the Lord were standing there ready to answer him, and he said, "I would ask Him to take away all ungodly desires and give me a clean heart." WOW, what an awesome request! I prayed and he felt the power of God go through him as I prayed. He told me that while he was in jail, he would read the booklet that I wrote and pray and he could see my face before him. The Lord's love is totally transforming. What an awesome blessing for the Lord to show me what He had done and was doing in this precious one. Glory be to God.

Journal Entry – February 2011

Friday, I registered with the Reinhard Bonnke School of Fire. The Lord led me to do this and provided the funds to do it. This is an in-depth and comprehensive course with five modules, twenty lessons per module, expected to take twenty to thirty weeks to complete, with exams after each module. A final exam and a certificate are awarded after successful passing of the exams.

I started the first module at 6:00 pm on Friday evening and continued non-stop, completing the final exam at 6:00 am Saturday. I slept for a couple of hours, and then after prayer continued non-stop and completed the entire course, including all the exams and the final exam, and submitted it before going to bed that same night. Glory be to God. Nothing is impossible with the Lord. Following is the result:

Course Certification –
Letter from Reinhard Bonnke's School of Fire - February 3, 2011

Thank you very much for submitting your final exam. We rejoice with you at the completion of the certificate course.

You have done an excellent job and received 100% in your final! Our congratulations on your successful completion of the certificate course!

Thank you for having taken our course on effective soul-winning and evangelism and for having been with us. It has been a privilege and blessing to have you "on board" and I hope the course has been of benefit to you.

It is our prayer that the School of Fire has become an ignition for a burning desire to reach out to the lost you come in contact with. We will pray for you and especially for the situation you are facing right now.

Sunday, I brought clothing to some families in need in Quebec, and when I arrived at one of the homes, a man was suffering from blood poisoning in his leg. He was in severe pain and his leg was swollen and very red. His wife brought me into his bedroom and he woke up when I entered the room. I laid my hands on his leg and asked the Lord to heal him.

After prayer, he got out of bed and I showed them the DVD testimony of Vi Schroeder, the lady that I met in the hospital. The presence of the Lord filled the room as they listened to her testimony.

When the DVD finished, this man told me that he had an experience with the Lord like this when he was fourteen years old, some forty-one years earlier. His wife was in tears as she heard him share his testimony with us.

When I got back home that evening and was getting ready to go to bed, the Lord told me that these people needed food. I phoned them and the lady started to cry when I told her that the Lord had told me this. I told her that they would have everything they needed "by this time tomorrow."

When I hung up the telephone, the Lord told me to get it for them. I went through my cupboards, fridge, and freezer. I packed what I could find, and the next morning I went to the local grocery store where there was a wonderful sale. I bought everything the Lord told me to and brought it to them.

There were more than ten boxes of food, and the people were overwhelmed when they saw what was in the boxes. It was exactly what they needed and the exact brands, too! Their two grown daughters were there and I sat and ministered to the entire family. They listened intently as I shared the Word of God with them, through the Scriptures.

The swelling in the father's leg was much improved, and the color was almost normal. He told me that he had slept very well the previous night, without pain. Glory be to God.

The love of God is so awesome! This entire family received the Lord Jesus with open hearts filled with gratitude.

Chapter 4

Mission Call to First Nations – 2008

Meeting Kenny Blacksmith

Kenny Blacksmith

I was teaching Bible study classes at the Northfield Pentecostal Church and was in week eleven of a twelve-week teaching on being led by the Holy Spirit, when one of the participants in the classes phoned me. He called to tell me that he had just led someone to the Lord and he was very excited. Then he said that this person was from Rapid Lake. As soon as he said, "Rapid Lake," I knew that I had to go there.

I can't explain it any other way than this overwhelming desire to go, and I shared this with him. He asked, "When"?

I said, "Right now!" In prayer that evening, the Lord gave me His promise from Luke 10:19 and I left for Rapid Lake the following morning at 10:30 am, October 19, 2008. When I arrived in Rapid Lake, the first person I met was Luke. This confirmed the Lord's promise to me: Luke 10:19 (NLT) *Look, I have given you authority over all the power of the enemy, and you can walk among snakes and scorpions and crush them. Nothing will injure you.*

Monique, a precious sister in Christ, called me one morning. The Lord told Monique to give me the phone number that was displayed on her television screen. I called, and it was the 700 Club. Lydia answered the call and when I told her that the Lord had called me to Rapid Lake and that Monique was directed by the Lord to give me their phone number, she fell to her knees at the other end of the line and said, "I know that this is God. I don't know who you are or where you are but I am on my knees." She began to pray as the Holy Spirit inspired her, and I remember that in her prayer she was asking the Lord to put a native pastor on my path.

When we got off the phone, I said to the Lord, "Lord, You already know who the pastor is. What is his name?" The Lord said very clearly, "Kenny Blacksmith." I then went to my computer and typed Kenny Blacksmith in Google and I found his website. I asked the Lord what He wanted me to see, and He directed me to Louise's testimony (Kenny's wife). I saw the call and what the Lord wanted me to do written in her testimony. I sent an email to Kenny. I did not know them and had never met with either Kenny or Louise.

The next day, I drove through the rain and darkness to Rapid Lake. As I approached Lac Roland, the presence of the Lord was so strong in my vehicle that I pulled over to the side of the road to pray. Suddenly I saw a vehicle pulled over in front of me, a dark-colored pickup with the signal light flashing. I saw a native man with a long ponytail get out and the Lord said, "Go and talk to him." Well, it was late, dark, and that was a secluded spot, but I did as the Lord told me to. I walked up to this man and asked him if he was from Rapid Lake, and he said, "No, I am from Mistissini."

I remembered that Kenny Blacksmith, according to the testimony on his website, was from the same place. I got excited and said, "Wow, do you know Kenny Blacksmith?" He touched my arm and said, "I am Kenny Blacksmith." I almost hit the pavement!

He was traveling across Canada, and as the Lord would have it, he crossed my path, just as the 700 Club prayer partner had requested. Praise be to God.

Chapter 5

RAPID LAKE

Casting out a Demon – October 20, 2008

This happened on my first day teaching in the native school in Rapid Lake. The teachers were gathered upstairs, preparing for an event, and all the children were with me in a room downstairs. The children were fighting and biting one another, and one little girl in particular was doing back flips on desks. She was four years old.

I asked the Lord, in the Spirit, not aloud, "Dear Lord, what is this?" Suddenly I realized that this was a manifestation of demons. I asked the Lord what to do, and He told me not to look at the little girl but to look at the demon in the girl. He told me that as soon as I saw it, to command it to come out of her, and not to come back and not to enter anyone else.

As I was talking to the Lord in the Spirit, everything became very quiet in the room. I realized that the demons could hear me talking to the Lord, and they knew they would have to go.

I noticed that the demon had the little girl backed into a corner of the room and she was staring at me. I walked over to her, as the Lord had directed me. I was looking into her eyes, waiting to see the demon. As soon as I saw it, I said in a loud voice with authority, "In the name of Jesus Christ of Nazareth, come out of her. Go and don't come back, and don't enter another." The little girl's head twitched twice to the side and she was free.

I walked back to my desk and sat down. I realized that no one had heard or noticed what just happened. All of the children were quietly playing. The little girl, who had just been set free, came over and sat on my lap. What a precious child.

It was break time and the children hurried outside to play, but I noticed that this little girl was having difficulty with her jacket. It was late in the fall and it was cold outside. I went over to her, knelt down in front of her, and asked her if she needed help.

She was struggling with the zipper on her "plastic jacket," and she said, "It's broken." This was the first time she had spoken. I noticed that the zipper was broken. It was plastic. She had no boots, no hat or mittens. This broke my heart. I said, "Dear Lord Jesus, I can't come back here without a coat for this little girl."

Shortly after this, people from many different places started giving me clothing to bring for these precious children. Praise His holy name forever.

Facial Healing

Wynonna – Four years after her healing

The evening of my second day in Rapid Lake, I heard a knock on the door. I opened the door and there was no one there. I knew that it was children. I said, "The door is open. You are welcome to join me." I went back to preparing supper and two young girls came in.

As I was speaking to them, I could feel the fire of God on my hands. I told them this and also said that one of them must need healing, otherwise I wouldn't be feeling this fire on my hands.

One of the girls said, "Can't you see her face? She just had a four-wheeler accident. She was thrown off and landed on her face." I placed my hands on the young girl (Wynonna) and she started to shout, "It's hot! It's burning!" I said, "Don't worry, dear, that's the power of God. He is healing you. When it stops, you will be healed." She fell onto the sofa and started laughing. The Lord healed her beautifully.

One of the teachers told me later that she thought this young girl would need corrective surgery on her face. But the Lord does a much better job and quickly. Praise His holy name. I saw this young girl recently, a young woman now, and she is beautiful.

Word of Knowledge – November 2008

I woke up one morning and suddenly had an odd pain shoot across my lower back. I said, "Dear Lord, there is nothing wrong with my back. What is this?" The pain left and didn't return. I went to the school as usual, but was a little early.

I was standing on the steps of the school when one of the teachers came by. She asked me to let the others know that she would not be coming in to work. She told me that she was going to the clinic. I asked her if she was okay, and she said that she had hurt her back.

Instantly, I realized that the pain that I had experienced that morning was the Holy Spirit showing me that He wanted to heal her back. I told her that she didn't have to go to the clinic because I had something for her better than that. I told her to go inside and find a place where we would not be disturbed, and that I would meet her there. She did as I said. I found her sitting in one of the empty classrooms.

She was sitting on a chair and I sat up on the desk in front of her. I shared with her what had happened that morning when I woke up, and asked her if she would let me pray for her. She said, "You don't have to, my back is fine now." She told me that while I was speaking, she felt heat where the pain had been, and by the time I asked if I could pray, she had already been healed. The Holy Spirit had already done it. Praise His holy name.

Tina's Dream of Jesus – October 2008
It was dark, raining, and late when I arrived in Rapid Lake. The person I was to meet was not home. I drove around the reserve and noticed a lady standing outside on a porch. I stopped to talk to her. Her name is Tina, an Italian lady who is teaching here in the government school. Not the native school where I am.

Tina invited me in, and of course the entire conversation until midnight was about the awesome goodness of God and knowing our precious Lord Jesus. She wasn't very open at first, however, before long she said she felt like praying, so we prayed together. She invited me to stay that night, and the next morning she told me of a dream she had had during the night, a dream of the Lord Jesus. He was there in her kitchen getting "milk" for her out of her fridge. She said she also dreamed of me. In the dream, she saw me with others, dancing, praising the Lord, and praying with her in her room. I showed her some Scriptures in the New Testament of pure spiritual milk in 1 Peter 2:2 and Hebrews 5:12-13, referring to spiritual nourishment, and told her that her Teacher is the Holy Spirit.

Tina came to see me three days later to ask what I did to her. I didn't understand what she meant. She told me that she had a back problem that caused severe pain. She had suffered with this for many years, but had just realized that the pain was gone. She was wondering when the pain had stopped and realized that it was the night that I had arrived in Rapid Lake and stayed in her home.

I told her that I didn't do anything, but the Word of God says that there are signs that follow those who believe the Gospel of the Lord Jesus Christ, and one of the signs is that we will lay hands on the sick and they will be healed. I reminded her that when we had prayed together, I held her hands and the Lord had healed her. She asked if I would pray for her knee also. I invited her in and prayed for her knee, and the Lord healed her knee also. Praise His holy name.

Tina invited me to visit the government school where she teaches. I met many people there, including the official Chief, and then I went to the native school to begin my work.

At lunchtime, a gentleman walked in the school and introduced himself as Kim, a Korean missionary. Kim is a member of a Korean church in Montreal, and was thrilled to find out that I am also a born again Christian and that I had moved here. He brought lunch with him; my favorite too: egg sandwiches and caramel cakes and apple juice. I was quite hungry, and so grateful to the Lord for sending lunch. He is so good.

Kim, the Korean missionary, has been here each day bringing lunch, and yesterday he brought a keyboard and we worshipped the Lord here in the school with the children and teachers. I shared the Gospel message, and three students believed.

On November 29th, a team, from Kim's church in Montreal are planning to come to Rapid Lake to hold a special meeting. Since they have difficulty with English and do not speak French, he asked if I would do the speaking. What an exciting time! It is the perfect time. The Lord is moving in a wonderful way here. Praise God. Praise Him!

Visitation from the Lord in a Dream - 2008

Children from Rapid Lake Reservation

One night, in Rapid Lake, I had a dream. I saw a little native girl sitting on the front steps of a house. She was crying. I put out my hand to her and asked her what was wrong, and she said that she was hungry. I took her by the hand and told her to come with me and I would find her something to eat. As I took her hand, I asked the Lord where I could find her something to eat, and He told me to turn around. When I did, the entire village was following me. Then I said to the Lord, "Dear Lord, I don't know where to find food for this little girl. How am I going to feed the whole village?" Then I woke up.

The next day, after teaching class, I stepped outside, and as soon as my foot touched the ground, I looked up and there was a man standing, looking right at me, and he said, "I have a truck load of food, where do you want it?"

I had never seen this person before. He told me that the Holy Spirit had directed him to come to that exact place. I know Richard now, an obedient brother in Christ. Later that evening, twenty-one children received Christ Jesus as Lord. What a wonderful Lord we serve. Glory be to God!

Revival Meeting - November 29th, 2009

There are three Chiefs on this reserve. This causes division in the community. The band office has been burned down. It's odd that it was the first building I went to when I arrived here. The door was open, but I didn't enter. This office was located right in front of the native school where I am teaching.

The room I am staying in this week has no heat. I use a blanket placed between the door and frame to keep it shut. But the Lord is so good. Tina sent her friend Yves to install a bolt on the door. Now I can keep the door closed when I am in there. He also brought me a little portable heater. Praise be to God, now I am very cozy.

After seven hours of praise, worship, prayer, and thanksgiving, all the children attending today's meetings in Rapid Lake received Jesus Christ as their Lord and Savior. Praise God!

The Lord sent a team of sixteen Korean missionaries, two native Christians from Oka, three Christian brothers from my home church in Northfield, Quebec, and three Christians from northern Ontario to Rapid Lake for revival meetings today, and the results were amazing. The Lord is moving in a mighty way here in northern Quebec. He is pouring out His Spirit and saving souls.

Raised from the Dead in Rapid Lake – April 2009

One night in Rapid Lake, the violence was extreme and I couldn't sleep. I could hear the fighting and screaming, and I was burdened for the precious children. I knew they must have been terribly frightened.

I asked the Lord to please do something. I didn't know what to pray for and I prayed for hours in tongues, then in English, pleading with the Lord to please do something. This went on until 4:46 am. I was in bed and wanted desperately to get up and go out into the street, but the Lord kept telling me to wait. Then I heard the most horrible scream I had ever heard, and at that very moment the Lord said, "Go!" I bolted out of bed and ran out into the street.

I saw a body on the ground about 200 feet away. It was dark, but I could see the body on the ground and a crowd of people surrounding the body. They were crying and one person knelt down, pressing on the chest of the body on the ground. I could see that the body was so swollen that the clothing was rolled up above the person's belly. I couldn't tell if it was a man or a woman.

When I reached the body, I fell to my knees and placed one hand on the person's forehead and the other in the air, and I looked up to heaven and in desperation said, "Dear Lord Jesus, we need Your help." When I said this, one of the elders who was present mocked me and questioned, "Jesus?" Then, with great authority, in a loud voice, I said, "Yes Jesus!"

Suddenly, the arms of the body stretched out from side to side and the person on the ground began to shake and tremble. The people surrounding the body suddenly went backward away from the body, and I could hear them saying, "This is not possible. We saw her head split open. She can't be alive." When I heard this, I knew that the person could hear them too, and I knew that the Lord had healed her and that she was okay.

I didn't want her to listen to them and be afraid, so I bent forward and whispered in her ear, "Don't listen to them. The Lord has healed you. You are okay." Her hand came up, but her eyes were closed, and she put her hand perfectly into mine and I wondered, "How does she see my hand?" Then with her other hand, she was reaching for my face, and she kept saying, "Dad," but her eyes were still closed. I wondered, "What does she see?"

Within minutes, she was up. There were no marks on her body and no blood on her or anywhere on the ground. She was filled with the joy of the Lord. Even the swelling was gone and her clothing was as it should be.

I recognized her as the assistant cook in the school. Her son was one of the students in my class. I had prayed for her son and he was healed just a couple of weeks prior to this. Shortly after this, the children in that school came to where I was staying and asked me how they could become Christians.

They all received Christ Jesus as their Savior and Lord. Yes, there is power in the name of Jesus to raise the dead. Praise Him forever.

Eggs – May 2009

While teaching as a volunteer in Rapid Lake, I would bring the most at-risk children home with me on weekends. One weekend, five of them came with me and I wanted to teach them to hear the voice of the Lord. They were to have a "treasure hunt." There were items on a list that they would have to find outdoors, and whoever found all of the items first would win. The children were trying to find these items on their own and were getting quite frustrated. I told them to ask the Lord to help them. They did. It was amazing to hear their excitement as the Lord showed them one by one. They all found the items at the same time. They were so amazed and excited. What a blessing for all of us.

It was time to prepare a meal. I was living by faith and had no income of any kind. I prayed and asked the Lord to help me feed the children. I found everything I needed to prepare spaghetti, their favorite meal. I was rejoicing that I had everything I needed. The children were playing outside. I opened the cupboard while the spaghetti sauce was simmering on the stove. I noticed a chocolate cake mix and chocolate icing, and I got so excited because the children love chocolate cake.

I wanted to be certain that I had all the ingredients before making the cake, and discovered that there were no eggs. I was a little disappointed, but was grateful that the children didn't expect to have dessert, and I told the Lord that I was grateful that we would have spaghetti.

I opened the fridge to get something, and right at eye level, sitting on a shelf, were four eggs. At the exact same time that I discovered the eggs, the children came in. They heard me shout, "Oh my God!" The children said, "What did Jesus do now?" I told them that the Lord had just supplied us with enough eggs to make a cake and one extra to make pancakes for breakfast the next morning.

We all rejoiced, thanked the Lord for this blessing, and we had chocolate cake for dessert. The Lord supplies all our needs and blesses us in so many amazing ways. What a loving, generous Father! Bless His holy name forever.

Journal Entry – June 2009

I received a phone call one evening in Rapid Lake, from Gary Fontaine, a brother in Christ. He phoned to tell me that one evening, as he was walking past a clothing store, the Lord prompted him to put his hand on the building and ask for clothing to be released for the children in Rapid Lake.

The Lord led Gary to a particular church a few days later. The pastor of the church told him that they had just received clothing from that store and they didn't know what to do with it. This brother told her how the Lord had led him to ask for clothing to be released from this store for the children in Rapid Lake. She told him to contact me and arrange for the clothing to be brought to Rapid Lake.

Rapid Lake is not close to Ottawa, where this church is. I asked the Lord how I was to get the clothing. Moments later, I received a phone call from a sister in Christ from Laval, Quebec, telling me that the Lord had told her to call and ask if I needed anything. Glory be to God.

I told her about the clothing and she offered to bring it to Bouchette, Quebec, and meet me there. When she arrived, she had one of her daughters with her. We had often prayed for this particular daughter to come back to the Lord. I was aware of her lifestyle, but I looked at her and asked her what she was doing. She said, "Nothing." Then I asked her if she would come and help me in Rapid Lake. Instantly she said, "Yes." I remember thinking, "Oh dear Lord, what have I done? She is not a good influence for the children that I am ministering to."

She got into my vehicle and we drove to Rapid Lake. I looked at her and said, "You know that I serve the Lord. You need to know that there is nothing of the world allowed in my home. All conversations are of the Lord. All music is Christian. Nothing is allowed that doesn't honor God and I don't want anything to interfere with the children growing in the knowledge of the Lord. Do you understand?" She said,

"Yes," then she said, "I knew that but I don't know why I said yes." She was referring to her having said yes to my asking her to come and help me in Rapid Lake.

On Tuesday evenings, many children would join me for Bible study and praise. This young lady had a very difficult time staying in the room while we praised God, and most of the time she would leave and not return before we finished. One Tuesday evening, she knocked on the back door, and one of the children opened the door slightly and said, "We are Christians and if you are a Christian come in, but if you're not, stay out!"

The door opened slowly and this young girl walked in. I was sharing a testimony of a miracle of God and she was clearly angry, but didn't say anything. When the children left, she sat at the table in front of me and said, "Well, He did do one miracle for me when I was little." She shared this with me when asked, but she was still angry. I said, "He has done many more, but you have forgotten."

She jumped up to leave and I said, "Melissa, you are not what you do." She took two steps and fell face down on the floor. When she got up, she placed her hand on the wall beside the doorway to her room and then she was gone. I thought, "Good Lord, what just happened?" I walked into her room and she was there, crying. I asked her what happened to her. She thought I was referring to her being face down on the floor. She said, "I tripped." Then I said, "On what?" She looked out from her room to the spot outside the door, and of course there was nothing there. Then I said, "And what happened at the door, I saw your hand on the wall and then all of a sudden you were gone. What happened there?" She looked at me, wide-eyed and said, "I went through the wall."

When she realized what she had said, she looked at me, expecting me to tell her what happened. I told her, "That was the Lord." She spent the following three days crying in her room. She repented and realized that the Lord is *real*. She has returned to faith in God through Jesus Christ our Lord. She has prayed for the sick and they have been healed and she loves the Lord.

I am in awe of God. He provides clothing for these precious children and He brought this precious one back to Himself, by the power of His Holy Spirit.

Encounter with the Police – August 2009

I returned to Rapid Lake after being away from the reserve for a weekend. The children came running to greet me as they always did. I noticed that two of the boys had a bow and arrows. This was unusual. I commented on this, but they didn't reply.

Shortly after the boys left, the cook from the school came over. She came to ask me if I had heard what had happened while I was away. I had not heard anything. She told me that some children had broken into the school and had taken some things. Some of the items taken were a bow and arrows. I thanked her for telling me and told her not to worry, that everything would be okay.

I love these precious children as though they were my very own, and I was very concerned. I prayed and asked the Lord to give me wisdom and asked Him what He would have me do about this.

While I was praying, the same two boys came back. They didn't have the bow and arrows with them. They stood next to me and I said, "Do you remember my teaching you about courage?" They answered, "Yes." Then I said, "Well, you know that doing something wrong does not take any courage, but doing something right does. When you have done something wrong and you want to make it right, it takes much more courage."

Then I told them, "If you ever do something wrong and you want to make it right, I will go with you and help you, because when you have someone with you it helps you to have more courage."

I walked inside to where the other children were. Moments later, one of the boys, "the smaller one," came inside and touched my arm. He looked up at me and said, "Me and Jim have done something wrong and we want to make it right." I asked, "Does Jim want to make it right too?" He said, "Yes." I went outside and asked Jim if he wanted to make things right and he said, "Yes." I asked if they wanted me to go with them and they both said yes. I told them to get in my car and I would meet them there.

I didn't have a plan. This simply unfolded a moment at a time. I had no idea what I was doing or what to do next. I simply followed the Holy Spirit. I went inside to get my car keys and the other children asked where I was going. They wanted to come with me. I realized that this was a huge thing for these boys and I did not want to embarrass them, so I told the other children that I was going with the boys for a few minutes and I would be right back.

When I got to the car, both boys were sitting in the back seat. I started the car, and as I pulled out I asked, "Where is the stuff?" They had not realized that I knew what they had done, but the oldest boy said, "It's at my house." I told them we were going to his house to get the stuff and he agreed. I stopped at his house and he went in alone and came back with the bow and arrows and some other things. He put them in the car and got back into the car.

As I drove out of his driveway, I told them that we were going to the police station. I would go into the police station first to explain to the police that they had done something wrong and wanted to make it right. They had both received Christ with me earlier, so I told them that the Lord was with them and told them not to be afraid, everything would be okay. They were doing the right thing, and the Lord would help them.

I went into the police station and told the officer about the situation. He said they did not have any report that the school had been broken into. Thank God. I told him that I was trying to teach the children to do the right thing and asked him to cooperate with me. He was very pleased and kind, and assured me that he would help. I went back to the car. The boys were sitting in the back. I told them that I had explained the situation to the officer and that he was very nice.

I instructed them to bring in the stuff. Tell the officer that they had done something wrong and wanted to make it right. Look the officer in the eyes and tell him the whole truth. Just as the boys got inside the police station, the officer had a phone call. While the officer was talking on the phone, the boys walked bravely past him and put all the stuff on the officer's desk.

When the officer got off the phone, the boys, looking directly at him, told him the whole story. The police officer wrote everything down without saying a word to them. When they had finished telling him the whole story, the officer told the boys that they had a friend in Rapid Lake. He told them he was their friend. He told them if they ever needed to talk to anyone about anything, to come and see him, any time, and he would be there for them.

These boys left that police station much taller, and I was so proud of them. The Lord's wisdom and love is truly amazing.

Shortly after this incident, two police officers stopped to speak to me. They said, "We don't know who you are or what you are doing here, but whatever it is, keep doing it, because we are seeing a difference." Praise be to God, His love never fails.

Chapter 6

MAIGANAJIK

Mission Letter to 700 Club Canada – July 7th, 2010

The Lord put a desire in my heart to establish a "safe place" for the children in this area. Volunteer Christian workers can come and minister the love of Christ as the Lord leads them.

I spoke to Ben about this last night. Ben is a member on the board of Directors at the Northfield Pentecostal Church. He also has a heart for the children living on the Reservations. Ben told me that there is a building for sale in the area.

This building will give us access to the community and a place to meet with those who need our help. The building needs work on the roof. But it's a start, and I trust that the Lord will provide the help we need to do this.

There is no electricity where the cabin is. We will need to find a generator. We will also need to get running water, sewage, and toilet facilities.

The Lord willing, I will travel to Rapid Lake this weekend. Can I tell them that we have the funding from CBA (The Christian Broadcasting Associates) to purchase the cabin?

The location is perfect. It's a safe location and only a thirty-minute drive from the main reservation of Rapid Lake.

The Lord has given us favor and the doors are open to share the Gospel of Christ Jesus and His love.

Thank you for your concern for the Native Children in Northern Quebec and for your willingness to help. Although I don't have the full plan yet, the Lord willing, we hope to find the building in good condition.

Children need a place where they can be safe, comforted, and encouraged in the Lord. I would appreciate prayer for this endeavor. We need the wisdom of God, plan of God, and workers. These children need all the help we can give them. They need to know God.

As Christians, the Lord has put His love in our hearts. We need to show them His love by expressing the love of God in our actions.

If there is any other way that the 700 Club could help, I would certainly appreciate it. May the Lord guide and direct you in this regard. The Lord be with you always, in Jesus' blessed name.

Letter from 700 Club Canada (CBA) – July 13, 2010
Hi Lorraine:

Glad things are coming along so well. Trust you are keeping well and strong.

You can certainly tell people that CBA is partnering with you and supplying the funds.

Letter to 700 Club Canada - July 16, 2010
Hi George,

I've attached the response from Pastor Jerry Ingravelle from the Northfield Pentecostal Church. This news arrives just in time. I am leaving in the morning for Rapid Lake and I am so excited to be able to bring them this awesome news, Glory to God—This is awesome news. They've been waiting for help and encouragement and the Lord is so faithful, His timing is always perfect, praise His holy name.

George, I am so grateful for your obedience to the Lord and your heart for these precious souls. This work will bring much glory to God through our wonderful Lord Jesus. What a tremendous blessing you are to this work. I thank the Lord for you and I thank you. Be blessed, precious brother, and may the Lord make His glorious face shine upon you and continue to bless the work of your hands.

Please let me know how you would like to proceed from here.

Letter from Northfield Pentecostal Church - July 16, 2010
Dear Lorraine:

The Board and I at Northfield Pentecostal Church are happy to announce that we would be happy to be involved in the purchase of the building for the children at Rapid Lake as a special project. Please forward these details to George Woodward at your earliest and God bless you for your passion and endeavors in His service. Should there be any further assistance, please do not hesitate to contact me at any time.
Jerry Ingravelle, Pastor
Northfield Pentecostal Church, Gracefield, Quebec

Report to 700 Club Canada - July 19, 2010

I returned from Rapid Lake last night at 9:30pm. The Lord went before me and prepared everything. The people welcomed me with open hearts, praise be to God.

I had many opportunities to witness the love of God through Christ Jesus as the children asked questions about Jesus. It was wonderful.

Your "Frontlines" News letter from July 2010 was in my mail box and I brought it with me and showed them. They read it and said, "This is really good." I then told them that 700 Club CBA were partnering with me by providing the funding to purchase the cabin. We and others, whom the Lord will send, can stay there and they can come. They are very moved by the love that CBA has shown to the poor and needy and for reaching out to help them in this way.

Ben and Maurice from the Northfield Pentecostal Church joined me. We brought clothing and gave it to them. One family in particular, consisting of a mom, dad, and six children under the age of twelve, were very grateful and amazed at the help they received. One of their children asked questions about Jesus, and they all listened intently to the message of Christ Jesus.

The area where the cabin is located is called Maiganajik in their local dialect, which is Algonquin. Translated to English, Maiganajik means "Wolf Territory." When they told me this, I remembered the scripture where our Lord told the disciples that He was sending them out as sheep among wolves.

Maiganajik is located at Le Domaine in Parc La Verendyre, Quebec. There are twenty families living there. They moved from the larger village of Rapid Lake in 1996 and lived in tents for two years. One person still lives in a tent, but the others have built cabins.

They wash themselves and their clothing in the lake and retrieve drinking water from a natural spring in the area.

Some have small generators to provide electricity when they are able to buy gasoline.

The Korean church in Montreal has built a community center and the door is left unlocked.

I felt the peace of God there and I believe that this is an answer to prayer. When it's the Lord's time, everything moves very smoothly and quickly.

Please let me know when we can expect the funding from CBA. I will travel to Rapid Lake again this weekend for a gathering, the Lord willing. It would be wonderful to finalize this purchase and start cleaning up the cabin.

If you have any questions, please feel free to contact me by email or by phone. May the Lord be with you and keep you in His perfect peace.

Letter from CBA 700 Club Canada – July 19, 2010
Hi Lorraine,

Sounds like you had a great trip. We can send the funds any time.

What I would like is a letter describing the mission, the house, its purpose, its ownership and its cost. Also who the cheque should be made out to and that 100% of it will go to the project. Please give full details of the location of the house and the mailing address of the church where the cheque is being sent.

Mission Report to 700 Club Canada - July 27, 2010

CABIN - MAIGANAJIK

Your cheque was received and the building has been purchased. Pastor Jerry Ingravalle arrived with Ben Lafreniere, from the Northfield Pentecostal Church on Saturday morning in Maiganajik and the transaction completed, praise God.

The community welcomed us. Michel, Guylaine, Melissa, Mark, Jerry, Ben and I have joined together in this work. We brought clothing for the people, toys for the children, and much needed supplies for the building.

Together we prayed for the people and dedicated the building to the Lord's work and others from the community joined with us in prayer.

The Elder in this community is a believer and related to George Nottaway. I believe that our being here and this outreach has come as an answer to her prayers for help. Glory be to God.

One family joined us Sunday afternoon and asked many questions about our Christian faith. Their hearts are open to hear, believe, and receive the Gospel of Christ.

Many do not know the Holy Spirit, and I pray that they will receive the baptism in the Holy Ghost.

Several members of the Korean church in Montreal came to the community. They prepared food for the community and gave free haircuts to any who wanted it. The young people in this group of fellow believers prayed with the children and spent time playing with them. They love these people also and they are loved by the people.

The Lord is working in the lives of these precious people. They are receiving His Love through you and all whom the Lord sends to them.

Thank you so much for all that you have done to make this possible. We could not have done this without your support. I pray that the Lord will bless you in multiple ways and keep your ministry strong.

I thank God for you and for all that you have done.

Bless His holy name. The children are coming and they are so precious. We brought toys for them as well as clothing. The joy of the Lord is also touching the hearts of these people. It's wonderful to hear laughter in this place. I look forward to all the Lord has planned for this place and I will keep you informed.

I shared the mission with them and the name of the building "700 Club - Christian Fellowship Center." They are deeply touched by your support and the love you have shown them.

The Lord willing, I will go back this weekend and expect that others will come also.

Mission: To help the First Nations peoples of Rapid Lake and surrounding territories by providing food and clothing, and show them the love of God. To share the full Gospel of Christ Jesus and the Kingdom of God with all who will receive.

Location of the House: Kilometer 333, Highway 117 North in Parc La Verendyre, on Jean Pierrier Lake, also known as Maiganajik.

Purpose of the House:

1. To provide a "safe place" for children where they will know and experience the love of Christ. A place where all who come will be comforted, encouraged, and trained in the way of the Lord.
2. Distribution of food and clothing.
3. A place where volunteer workers can stay and minister to the needs of the people.

Once purchased, the house will be dedicated to the Lord's work and used for His purposes. Volunteer Christian workers from any and all denominations are encouraged to help and are welcome to use the premises as needed to minister to the needs of the people. We also have access to the local community center for ministry to the community at large. The building will be named "700 Club - Christian Fellowship Center."

Cost of the House: One thousand dollars.

The cheque for the house should be made out to Northfield Pentecostal Church - Rapid Lake Building Project. 100 percent of the funds will go to this project.

Letter to Northfield Pentecostal Church - December 2010

Hi Ben, Thank you for the nice message you left on my phone. I was in Maiganajik this weekend and someone broke open the door. I was wondering if you could put a hook on it like you did before, so the wind doesn't blow the door open.

There's lots of snow. I shoveled a bit. If anyone needs to use the generator, the key is hanging up on the key rack inside. I brought the gas can home to fill up with diesel fuel for Christmas. There is not very much fuel in it right now and it's important that it doesn't run empty because it's hard to start.

I didn't get any news from Amos, but he is more than welcome to stay at the cabin. There's lots of wood, he should be very comfortable there. The Lord willing, I will spend Christmas in Maiganajik

When you get together with Amos and Richard, would you please join together in prayer for Dylan? He told me that he takes drugs to ease the pain in his heart from all the abuse that he suffered. I have such a burden in my heart for this little boy. I've been praying that the Lord will intervene and deliver him and heal his precious heart and keep him safe.

Thank you, Ben, you are precious brother in Christ, may the Lord go before you and make your way successful.

Mission Report to 700 Club – September 2010

My heart is overflowing with gratitude as I write this update. The little boy who was on my heart in June, Dylan Maranda, just phoned me. He is now living in a place called Winnaway.

Dylan has been placed by the courts in a Christian home. I spoke to the Christian sister who is taking care of him. They love Dylan and he is very happy. Praise God for this wonderful answer to prayer. Dylan is so very precious. The cabin in Maiganajik came because of prayer regarding Dylan. Glory be to God.

Today, I received an invitation to speak to the Catholic Women's League at Our Lady of Fatima Catholic Church in Renfrew on the 18th of October. This came about because of the clothing and food distribution in Maiganajik. One of the ladies from this church, Mabel, heard about this work. She contacted the Catholic Women's League and they want to help.

This is an awesome opportunity to share my testimony with them. They also asked for copies of the booklet that the Lord had me write, "My Best Friend Can Be Your Best Friend Too." The Lord is pouring out His Spirit in an amazing way. What a time to be alive. What a marvelous opportunity to share the goodness of our Lord and Savior Jesus Christ.

Last weekend, the Lord gave me favor with a U-Haul dealer. They rented me a van to take the food, clothing, and toys to Maiganajik. I picked the van up on Friday at 4:30pm and returned it at 5:00pm on Sunday, and they only charged me for one day, plus 582 kilometers. Praise God. Thursday, it didn't look possible, but after being paid for the homes that I cleaned on Friday, I had enough money to pay for it. I Praise God for His provision and favor.

Two more community members received Jesus in Maiganajik this weekend. One man received healing in the name of Jesus on Saturday evening. Glory to God.

Clothing is steadily coming in and the Lord has been giving me direction as to where to purchase food at low cost, and He is providing me with the work necessary to pay for it.

Last week, I cleaned twenty-two homes in five days with His help. The Lord gives me the strength and when the work is finished I'm not even tired. It feels as though I've done nothing. He is teaching me to work from His place of rest, in Him, how awesome.

The Lord is bringing more and more believers alongside to help and I am so grateful.

Letter from CBA President George Woodward – September 2010
Hi Lorraine.

Thank you for the great testimonies. The 700 Club is privileged to be connected with a woman like you that has such love and compassion for others.
God bless you.
George Woodward, President, CBN Canada

Mission Report to 700 Club Canada – December 2011

Help is pouring in. It's truly amazing to see the goodness of God as He moves in the hearts of people to give. The Catholic Women's League (CWL) is preparing Christmas gifts for me to bring to the children of Maiganajik and Rapid Lake. Others are baking and preparing gifts to give to all the families for Christmas.

At the moment, I have enough toys to give to each child in the reservations where I go. Praise God for His goodness and the obedience of those who are answering the call to give. Glory be to God.

The ministry in Maiganajik is going very well. Hearts are changing as we minister the word and love of God to the people.

Last weekend, a local man came to the center when I was alone. He told me that when I first came to Maiganajik, he hated me. He said that he thought that we were crazy people. Especially when he saw people follow me down to the Lake to be baptized. He had come to tell me that now he knows we speak the truth. He told me that he had changed his mind about us from seeing us "love one another." He cried and told me that he wants to have what we have.

I told him we have Jesus in our hearts and he can also. He knows that he needs the Lord and he wants to turn from his own way of living and live the life we live.

The Spirit of the Lord is reaching into hearts and drawing them to God through the Lord Jesus Christ. Awesome, just awesome! What an awesome God we serve.

Mission Report to 700 Club – January 2011

Much has happened since the December update I sent. I spent New Year's Eve at a local church, WCCA, in Kinburn, Ontario, with brothers and sisters in Christ. The service started at 7:00 pm. No one wanted to leave because the presence of the Lord was so awesome. What a wonderful way to spend New Year's Eve, and what an awesome blessing to be in the presence of our Lord together with the Body of Christ.

Trips to Maiganajik are less frequent in winter. It is costly and I don't always have the funds to go. This is the case for the others who come also. The roof in the cabin has been leaking and Michel, who looks after the repairs and renovations, is also finding it increasingly difficult to do what needs to be done because of a lack of funds.

Michel Bervaldi

Michel phoned to explain his circumstances and to tell me he was waiting for funds to come in, which would enable him to go and repair the roof. I prayed with him over the phone, asking the Lord to provide what was needed for Michel to go and do the necessary repairs. The Lord is faithful.

I met Michel in Maiganajik last weekend. He told me how he was led by the Holy Spirit to a dumpster in Montreal.

The dumpster contained all the wood that he needed. Praise God.

Michel spent seven days at the cabin and was able to insulate the ceiling and repair the roof. Glory and praise be to God.

More people received healing in their bodies and we had many opportunities to witness to the community.

Mission Report to 700 Club Canada – December 2010

This photo was taken in my home in Renfrew last Saturday. The family in the center of the photo received Christ as their Lord and they were baptized in the Lake in Maiganajik this summer. The ladies sitting beside them are Mabel Proulx on the left and Darlene Barr on the right, with her Granddaughter from Renfrew. Mabel and Darlene have been a tremendous help to the missions. They gather clothing, toys, and household items for the First Nations People.

The family from Maiganajik left with a school bus filled with toys, clothing, household items, and food to bring back to their community. What a tremendous blessing.

Today, when I arrived home from work, I found more than sixty gifts, individually wrapped and ready to give to the children for Christmas. They were dropped off by the President of the Catholic Women's League in Renfrew. Wow, I was speechless when I saw this. Glory to God. It's truly amazing to see the help pouring in for these precious people.

Last night, I drove a van full of new believers to the local Teen Challenge for a prayer meeting. We were blessed beyond measure by the presence of our wonderful Lord.

Mission Report to 700 Club Canada - Christmas 2010 in Maiganajik

Christmas 2010 in Maiganajik was awesome. The Lord healed three people; the first was a lady who was sick in bed when I arrived Christmas Eve. I went to her home and sat beside her as she lay in bed and prayed, quoting from the scripture in Mark 16:15 and these signs shall follow those who believe, they shall lay their hands on sick people and they will get well.

She was made well and attended the Christmas Day gathering the next day. Glory to God. This lady's son came to visit me at the cabin on Christmas morning. He was having difficulty breathing. I quoted the same scripture to him and then laid hands on him and he was healed.

The next day, a man took an overdose of prescription drugs and had been drinking for days. The community expected to have to take him to the hospital to have his stomach pumped. I told them that God was stronger than anything this man had taken. His face was ashen (gray), and he was losing consciousness.

I placed my hands on him and started praying in tongues. Suddenly, I remembered a phone call from Michel. He had phoned me the morning that I was leaving for Maiganajik and told me that he had a vision of me that morning. He said, in the vision he saw the Lord anointing me and saw me holding up a glass of water to the Lord.

I got a glass of water and held it up to the Lord and asked Him to bless the water and use it to flush out the effects of what this man had consumed. I gave the glass of water to him and told him to drink it, in the name of the Lord Jesus Christ. He drank it.

I got the Bible and placed it in front of him and instructed him to read scripture out loud from the books of Titus and Psalms. He said, "I can't read without my glasses." I prayed once more, asking the Holy Spirit to help him. He then opened the Bible that I gave him and started to read. He read it perfectly, out loud, and the Holy Spirit gave him revelation.

Before finishing these scriptures, his whole countenance changed and his mind had cleared. Glory be to God.

Also on Christmas day, I attended the community gathering and gave gifts to all the children that were donated by the CWL in Renfrew. We had a wonderful, joyful Christmas.

I had prayed, asking the Lord for roads to be clear for this trip. From the moment that I prayed until this time, the roads are clear. Praise be to God.

I didn't have the means for this trip and was not sure if I would be able to go, but God is so faithful. The very morning that I was to leave, a cheque arrived in my mailbox. It was more than enough to cover the entire cost of the trip. Praise be to God. What a wonderful Father we have! What amazing love! Glory be to God.

I had prayed for an opportunity to witness to a specific man, and the opportunity came on Monday. He came to the cabin Monday afternoon because he needed some insulation for his camp. I gave it to him and then offered him a coffee. He accepted the coffee, sat, and listened for four hours to my testimony of the Lord Jesus Christ. I could see him changing as he received the message with an open heart.

Maranda was there with us, and she testified to him also. What a blessing to be able to testify of our precious Lord Jesus and have a child testify also. We plant the seed of God's Word and He makes it grow. Praise His holy name.

On my way home, I met a van full of people from the community. They had just come from helping a lady to get her vehicle out of a creek. They stopped me, and one of them said, "We've never met anyone like you. You give so much. We can't thank you enough for all that you have done." I told them that it's the Lord who provides for them. He gives to them, through me. Everything they have received is from Him.

They asked me to come back to attend their New Year's celebration. The Lord willing, that's where I will be. Thanks to all of you for your help and encouragement in this work.

Mission Report to 700 Club Canada – July 2011

Clothing, toys, and household items are pouring in. Half of my garage is filled with toys! I've had to contact someone with a truck to help bring it here. It's truly amazing to see all of this come in. Every weekend my car is full, but what's coming in now will take a U-Haul truck! In two days, all of this came in.

The Lord told me to stop at a little gas station before going to clean my Wednesday night homes. When I entered the gas station, the cashier said, "Can you go to 97 Libbey Road?" I said yes, then asked what for, and she replied that there was a garage full of toys for me. When I went to clean other homes today, I was given clothing, bags of clothing, and there is more on the way. More and more people are offering to help. It's wonderful, but I need a means of getting all of this to the people.

As you know, I clean houses and this work provides me with the means to travel each weekend to Maiganajik and bring food, clothing, and supplies. With the way the Lord is moving on the hearts of people to give, it will take more than my car to get these things there.

Please join me in prayer for the Lord to provide the necessary means to get all of this to the people. I can hardly wait to see the faces of the children when they see all of this!

The Lord is blessing these people in an amazing way. How awesome is His love for His children. I am getting to know Him more and more as I witness the outpouring of His amazing love. Glory, honor and praise to our Father through Christ Jesus our Lord! What a time to be alive!

Mission Report to 700 Club Canada – August 2010

The community of Maiganajik is responding, in a marvelous way, to our presence here. They love to hear our testimonies and they welcome us with open hearts and arms.

We have been there every weekend and are heading back today, the Lord willing. The roof has been repaired. Mark brought and installed a new wood stove with an insulated chimney. He also brought and is installing maple hardwood flooring.

This weekend, Mark will put up a partition to make two bedrooms. Mark has been coming to help and he has been sleeping on a sofa in the living area of the cabin. Anyone who has seen this sofa knows that he needs a bed! Once a partition has been put up, he can have a room and be able to sleep in a bed.

Ben and Maurice came to get water, but rather than get water they introduced two community members to Christ. They found one of them walking on the highway. He had a rope, and when Ben and Maurice stopped to give him a ride, this man told them that he was going to hang himself. Ben and Maurice cast a demon out of this man and then proclaimed the Gospel to him. He accepted Christ Jesus as Lord and threw away the rope. Glory be to God!

Richard and Amos, two Christian brothers from Arden, Ontario, came in on Sunday and stayed at the cabin. They brought wood for one of the community members to fix his house. The community not only welcomed them but made a "feast" for them. During the feast, Richard felt the Holy Spirit prompting him to worship. He took out his guitar and Amos joined him in worship.

The presence of the Lord was so intense that one of the community members stood up and said, "I need to repent. Tell me how to repent." Glory to God! The harvest is truly ripe and it's time to reap!

Guylaine emailed me with news that Michel, Raymond, and Peter are coming at the end of August to install windows and insulate the floor for the winter. With the leading of the Holy Spirit, much more than that will take place. Praise God.

The Lord is so faithful. This week, from my tithe account, I was able to purchase a one thousand watt generator and a power pack. With these, we will be able to have electric lights in the cabin. The power pack will continuously run a CD player for thirty-five hours. It can easily be recharged while the generator is operating. Now we can have worship music playing in the cabin, and lights. I had enough money in this account to purchase a BBQ and enough food to feed the people, buy clothing for them, and a bicycle. Imagine, I clean homes, and yet with the Lord all this is possible. Praise, honor and glory to our wonderful Lord!

We are all members of the Body of Christ and we need one another. All are equally important. As we let the Lord lead, wonderful fruit is produced and the Kingdom of God steadily advances. Each of us using the gifts the Lord has given us, for the profit of all.

Mission Report to 700 Club Canada – August 2010

The Lord graciously provided, through the 700 Club in Canada, a cabin in Maiganajik, a thirty-minute drive from the First Nations Reserve in Rapid Lake. We named it the 700 Club Christian Fellowship Center. The first week, two precious children were healed.

The first one to be healed was a seven-year-old boy. He came into the center crying and showed me his hand. He couldn't open his hand. I asked him if he knew Jesus. He had no idea who Jesus was. I told him who Jesus is and then told him that Jesus would heal him. I took his hand in mine and asked the Lord to heal him. Instantly he stopped crying and opened his hand. He received the Lord and was baptized in the lake the following week. Praise be to God.

The following day, I heard another child crying. She came crying to the center and was crying so hard that she couldn't talk. She also had hurt her hand, and she came to me. When I looked at her hand, I saw a hole where the knuckle of her thumb should be.

The first thought that came to mind was *hospital,* but there are no hospitals in this area. I took her hand in mine and looked up to the Lord and said, "Dear Jesus, I need the power of the Holy Spirit for this." As I said this, I could feel something move beneath my hands. I took my hands away and could see that her hand was perfectly normal. Glory be to God.

These children did not know me. They had never seen me before, yet they came running to me, rather than anyone else. The Lord obviously drew them to Himself through me. They are now precious children of God and they are experiencing the wonderful goodness of God.

The 700 Club has been constantly alongside, helping in this wonderful work, and I thank God for their obedience and love for these precious First Nations people. The Lord is bringing the prodigals home. Praise His holy name.

Mission Report to 700 Club Canada – August 2010

**700 Club Christian Fellowship Center –
"Cabin" in Maiganajik**

Twenty-two people came to the cabin on Sunday, August 15th, 2010 to be baptized in the lake. After sharing the Word with them regarding baptism, they followed me to the lake and were baptized in the name of Jesus for the remission of sins. I prayed for each one individually to receive the baptism of the Holy Spirit. What a glorious sight. One of the children captured the entire event on video.

The goodness of God is being poured out in Maiganajik. Christian brothers and sisters are coming from many different places as they are led by the Holy Spirit. It is truly an awesome sight to behold as the Body of Christ joins together as one in this work.

The community members are witnessing the love of God in action. The Lord said in John 13:35, *"By this all men will know that you are my disciples, if you love one another."* This blesses the heart of our Father, the Lord Jesus Christ, and the Holy Spirit.

When I arrived in Maiganajik on Saturday, Ben and Maurice from the Northfield Pentecostal Church were finishing work on the chimney. This chimney was given to us by someone I met at the Little Brown Church, in Renfrew, Ontario.

Maurice, led by the Holy Spirit, was moved to share the Gospel with a family. They believed the message and accepted Jesus as Lord. Maurice's testimony is also on a video that I sent to you.

A little later that day, three more Christian brothers and Melissa, who worked with me in Rapid Lake in 2008, arrived. They are members of a house church that meets in Laval, Quebec, and in Casselman, Ontario.

They brought brand new windows, doors, building materials, insulation, a new toilet, sink, vanity, two picnic tables (built on-site), a water pump with tank, a shower, 5500 diesel generator, which will operate everything we have, and food, food, and more food, to the glory of God.

I had to sit down when I saw everything. I was totally overwhelmed. What an amazing sight, and what glory this brings God. The village witnessed this in amazement also. This community is witnessing the love of God in action among His precious children. God is so good!

I asked Michel if he could nail two nails on the board that I had placed on top of a little fridge. I was using it as a counter and needed to keep it in place. Rather than put the nails in to keep the board secure, they built me an eight-foot counter. Complete with hooks to hold pots and pans, a full-length shelf, and shelves for dishes. Then they made a built-in place for the little fridge and set the fridge inside. Glory to God, this is perfect! Now I can prepare and cook meals in one place. Wow, I am so grateful.

While I was shopping for supplies needed for the weekend, I saw a large can of Nescafe instant coffee for $7.98. I realized that this money would be better spent on bread and other food for the people.

When Melissa came to the center, she said that the Lord told her to buy me the exact same coffee. I really like Nescafe instant coffee, and the tin is practical. It keeps the mice out. The wonderful goodness of our Father! He knows that I like this and He had my precious sister buy it for me. How awesome is His loving kindness.

The Lord also put it on the heart of two brothers to give me precise amounts of money. It totaled the exact amount that I needed to cover my rent. This is the love of God. He sees everything and knows what we need and gives it to us at just the right time. Yes, the Lord supplies all of our needs all the time. Praise His holy name. He does this through the obedience of His children at times.

We spent Saturday and Sunday together in fellowship, worship, and prayer. When everyone left on Sunday, one of the families in the village came to fellowship with me until late in the night.

I left on Monday afternoon in total awe of the goodness of our Father. There is so much more to tell you, but it's getting late and I still have four more houses to clean tonight.

Once again, I thank you and thank the Lord for you. Your help has made this possible. I want you to know that we truly appreciate your purchasing this building for this work. Your help is bringing glory to God, souls into the Kingdom, and the love of God is being seen and felt in this place.

Mission Report to 700 Club Canada – September 2011

As I was preparing a DVD for you, I received a phone call from another brother in Christ. He told me that the Lord just told him to go to Maiganajik on Thursday. His name is Roland Meloche, he is a retired carpenter from Orleans, Ontario. I met Roland while speaking at a house church in Casselman. The timing is perfect. Michel has been in Maiganajik for two weeks doing renovations and he could sure use the help. Praise God.

Roland has come alongside to help with the ministry to the First Nations communities in Northern Quebec. Roland travels frequently to stay at the 700 Club Christian Fellowship Center in Maiganajik, also known as the "cabin." During his last trip to Maiganajik, Roland discovered a young man in the cabin who had no food. Roland welcomed him to stay and shared his food with him. He shared the Gospel with him and prayed for him.

After receiving prayer, this young man was filled with the peace that only Christ our Lord can give. He was at the right place at the right time. Praise be to God for placing this young man on Roland's path to hear the Good News.

The "cabin" is the Lord's place, and His purpose is being carried out there. I thank God for Roland's obedience to go, and for the 700 Club partnering with us. Many have been ministered to and have received Christ, and the work continues.

The Lord willing, I will travel to Maiganajik on the 24th of September, 2011, with Debbie and Roland. We want to bring much-needed supplies, food, and clothing for the winter.

Mission Report to 700 Club Canada – September 2011

Thank you so much for your prayers. We felt them. This was a glorious trip. The presence of God was felt in a tangible way. Even animals praised the Lord as we praised Him in the open air.

The children came every day to the cabin. One afternoon, a child came along as we were sitting outside. He was looking for his cat. His cat ran away from his home and came to the cabin. I asked him if he knew Jesus and he said no. Then I asked him if he knew who we were, and once again he said no. I told him that we were Christians. I asked him if he would like to know the Lord like we do, and he said yes.

I shared the Gospel and read to him from the 'little book,' entitled "My Best Friend can be your Best Friend too." He listened intently and we testified about the Lord and how he had healed children in Maiganajik. I asked him if he was ready to receive Christ as His Lord and he said yes. I prayed with and for him, and he was so excited. Praise be to God for drawing this precious little one unto Himself. Glory be to God.

What an experience to see precious children coming to God through Christ, our wonderful Lord.

The peace and presence of God in this place is so awesome. There are wonderful changes taking place here. It is not the same at all. The road has been fixed and is smooth to drive on. We can now access the fresh water spring by vehicle. Praise be to God. A logging company did the road work, but we know that our Lord had them do it. Praise be to God.

Many people were sick when we arrived, but after prayer they are all well. Glory be to God.

It is such a tremendous blessing to have Roland and Debbie with me in Maiganajik. I am so grateful that the Lord sent them alongside to help. Roland travels once a month to Maiganajik bringing supplies, witnessing to and praying for the people. He helps them with carpentry work on their homes. Roland has a gentle, quiet spirit. The children and people welcome and love Roland. He is perfectly equipped for this work. Praise be to God.

Debbie stays with me in Renfrew and helps me with everything. What a marvelous blessing. She loves the Lord completely and we enjoy staying in the presence of our precious Lord 24/7. Glory be to God. I am so grateful that the Lord sent her.

Debbie and I received Christ together as little children, and now together we witness to other children. It warms our hearts to see that the Lord is using us in this way. We know the difference the Lord makes in a life surrendered to Him, and have known from childhood.

Nothing in this world compares to the love, mercy, and tenderness of our precious Lord, who is always with us. Glory be to God.

Mission Report to 700 Club Canada – February 2011

KOKOM - Celebrates her 81st Birthday in Maiganajik

The Lord is so good. This weekend I was able to bring lots of food and clothing to Maiganajik.

The elder in the village celebrated her 81st birthday on Sunday. We cleaned the Community Center for them. We helped to set up the tables and chairs for Kokom's birthday party, and Michel prayed for one of the women. She testified that she felt better after receiving prayer. Praise be to God.

Show Them My Love

    I spent most of Saturday with Maranda. She is a precious little girl, with faith in God and she is growing in the knowledge of the Lord. When I brought the food to her family, there were many people in their home and they were all surprised because they had been talking amongst themselves about what they wanted to have to eat. They had mentioned the exact items I brought for them. I told them that the Lord had instructed me on what to get, as He knows everything.

    What an awesome witness when this happens. They know that there is no other explanation. Glory be to God.

Maranda

Maranda (left) with her siblings..............

Michel did a wonderful job insulating the cabin, and he is spending another five days in Maiganajik, ministering to the needs of the people. I thank God for his faithfulness in this work. He truly has a servant's heart and has sincere love and compassion for the people.

The Lord has provided me with more work. One of my customers is a home builder. I clean eight of their model homes twice a week at night. They have hired me to work in their office on the weekends as well. I started last week. They have agreed to give me one weekend off per month to go to Maiganajik. I thank God for this additional work because it enables me to cover my own expenses, travel to Maiganajik, and purchase food for the people there.

This new job also gives me more opportunities to witness, to co-workers and customers. Praise God. Thank you for your prayers, help, and encouragement. May the Lord be with you and keep you in His perfect peace.

Val D'Or - Mission Report to 700 Club Canada – June 2011

The Lord is so faithful. My new job has provided many wonderful opportunities to share my faith in God through our Lord and Savior Jesus Christ. Within the last two weeks, my employer opened a new office in Val D'Or.

If you recall, when I first received the call of God to go to Rapid Lake, I spoke with one of the 700 Club prayer partners who was from Val D'Or, Quebec. She told me that she has been praying for many years for the people there. My employer has asked me to work in the Val D'Or office.

Many of the children who received Jesus as Lord are now living in Val D'Or. Please keep me in prayer for the Lord to reach many through His saving grace and power of the Holy Spirit.

My employer will pay all expenses associated with my travel. Glory be to God for this awesome opportunity. We serve a MIGHTY GOD.

Lac Simon - Mission Report to 700 Club Canada – June 2011

I put 1218 kilometers on the van during the trip to Val D'Or this week. On my way, I stopped in at Maiganajik. Val D'Or is 180 kilometers further north from Maiganajik. While driving to Val D'Or, I noticed the sign for Lac Simon.

I have wanted to go to Lac Simon since I heard about the many suicides on that reserve, but didn't know where it was located. As I passed the sign to turn off to Lac Simon, I told the Lord that I would really love to go there. I told Him that it would be easier if I knew someone there.

I arrived in Val D'Or and I went to the office to meet with the person who works in the office there. After listening to him speaking, I felt that he was a Christian. I asked him if he was and he said yes. He asked if I would like to listen to some music while I worked. He asked me what type of music I would like to listen to. I told him that I love listening to Christian music and that's the only type that I like. He put on Sirius Christian Music, 'The Message.' Our Val D'Or office is shared with a car dealership. All the staff heard 'The Message' on the radio station throughout the entire week. Praise be to God. It was awesome.

I left early on Thursday and picked up a hitchhiker on the highway just outside of town. He said his name was Douglas and he was going to Lac Simon. As he told me this, his cell phone rang and the ring tone was a Christian song. I told him that I was a Christian also and that I knew the Lord had set this meeting up. I had wanted to go to Lac Simon, but didn't know anyone there. He told me that the new chief in Lac Simon was a Christian lady by the name of Salome.

When he told me her name, I remembered meeting her in Montreal two years ago with Joseph Lafontaine. I asked him if he would come with me to see her. As I asked him, his cell phone rang again. He looked shocked. It was her, Salome, sending him a text message telling him that they were having a prayer meeting that evening and she wanted him to join them.

He told her that he was with me and that I wanted to meet with her. She agreed. How awesome is our wonderful Lord!

I met with eight Christians in Lac Simon. They meet every Wednesday evening. This Thursday evening meeting was an exception. Glory be to God. They had postponed the meeting so that Douglas could be there. We had a wonderful time together! What a blessing to meet and fellowship with Christian brothers and sisters! The love we share is so amazing. Glory be to God.

They invited me to join them on Wednesday evenings whenever I am in the area. Lac Simon is only a twenty-minute drive from Val D'Or. Praise be to God.

I continued on to Maiganajik and arrived just before dark. I had received a text message from them. They were in need of food and I brought them what they needed. I witnessed to some people and they listened intently as I told them what the Lord had been doing.

The Lord put it on my heart to stay there overnight. The next morning, two of the people I had witnessed to the previous night seemed even more intent to listen as I witnessed to them about Jesus our Lord and His amazing love. As I spoke, I noticed the presence and the power of the Holy Spirit was increasing, and I waited on the Lord to know what He would have me do.

I wasn't getting any direction and stood up to leave. As I got up, the two men who were really intently listening got up also. Both of them said, "We need the Lord in our lives." One of them said that he had wanted this all his life. I shared the entire Gospel message of salvation with them. I asked them if they were ready to give their lives to God and receive Jesus in their hearts as Lord, and they both said yes.

I prayed for them and then they prayed and received the Lord Jesus Christ. Two more Christian brothers, glory be to God. One of these men is Maranda's dad. Praise be to God. Now her mom and dad are Christians.

I gave them resources that the 700 Club so graciously gave me. This is a tremendous help and exactly what they need. I thank you so much for supplying these.

There is much work to do, in Maiganajik, Rapid Lake, and Lac Simon. I pray that the Lord will send more workers. The doors are open and the harvest is truly ripe.

The Korean missionaries have been faithfully planting the seed of the Word and the Lord has made it grow. It is time to harvest.

Mission Report to 700 Club – July 2011

Roland Meloche

The Lord blessed us with perfect weather. Roland spent the week and did much-needed repairs to the cabin, as well as building a deck for one of the community members. The children love Roland and I thank God for his obedience to come and minister to the needs of the people.

In June, I prayed asking the Lord for simple English Bibles to give to the new Christians. One day shortly thereafter, I heard an announcement on a Christian radio station. They were offering free, plain English Bibles, available by Internet at lifeonline.fm. Praise be to God.

I went to their website and requested that the Bibles be sent directly and individually by mail.

While I was in Maiganajik this week, Maranda was the first to receive hers by mail. She began reading it to the other children. What a wonderful blessing. The others arrived throughout the week, glory to God.

Show Them My Love

The children spent their days and evenings with us. We had many opportunities to minister.

One day, Shawna, one of the children had a severe nosebleed. After laying hands on her and praying, it stopped, instantly. The children were amazed. This gave me another opportunity to witness about the power in the name of Jesus our Lord.

Another man, who said he didn't like 'Christians,' came to the cabin one evening to mock us. After witnessing to him, he began to weep and poured out his heart to me. He came back the next morning and told me that when he woke up that morning, all he could think about were the words I spoke to him the previous evening. He came with a guitar and began playing and singing Christian worship songs "from his heart."

The Lord is awesome, and what a blessing to see the Word of God, spoken in love, with the power of the Holy Spirit changing hearts.

Maranda and her dad planted a garden and it's growing beautifully. They also have two pigs. They told me that Ben, from the Northfield Pentecostal Church, blessed them with chickens. They are doing very well. They have fresh eggs every day and share with the rest of the community. The chickens had little ones. Maranda is very happy about this.

Patrick connected a fire pump from the lake to the community center. The pump was donated by Rock and Louise, a Christian couple from Gracefield, Quebec. This makes water from the lake available for washing, showers, and any other needs they have for running water.

Patrick also set up a large diesel generator at the community center that provides power for the nearby homes, including the 700 Club Fellowship Center.

Louisiana Pacific came to fix the main road into Maiganajik, as well as a road leading to the natural spring water supply. We can now drive to the spring to get water. Praise God for this wonderful blessing.

Monique sent me a bed with bedding, and it is so comfortable. I am very grateful for her generosity, and I thank God for this blessing also.

I thank God for the ability to bring in lots of food and clothing for the community and for the van that the 700 Club so graciously helped me purchase. It's perfect for this work.

Clothing, toys, and household items continue to steadily pour in. It's difficult to leave. I love these precious people so much and pray for another opportunity to go soon. Maranda's parents have agreed to let Maranda come and spend time with me in Renfrew soon, and I look forward to this very much. She loves to listen to the Word and testimonies of Christ Jesus our Lord.

Thanks to all of you for your prayers, encouragement, love, and support. When I think of you, I am reminded of these words spoken by our Lord Jesus Christ as recorded in John 13:35, *"Your love for one another will prove to the world that you are my disciples."*

May the Lord continue to strengthen and uphold us in His love, as we share freely the blessings He has bestowed upon us.

First Nations Blessed by 700 Club Canada Team – August 2012

700 Club Canada Visit Maiganajik

The Lord arranged for the 700 Club Team to visit and bless the First Nations people. I am not certain they realize how many people have been blessed as a result of their obedience to the Lord's call to come and help these past two weekends.

Through the partnership of the 700 Club in Canada, we now have a permanent building in Maiganajik. We are able to reach many communities in this area.

The 700 Club Team arrived with school backpacks filled with school supplies and goodies for the children in Rapid Lake, Maiganajik, Cabonga, the "Airport Community in Le Domaine," Maniwaki, Kazabazua, Danford Lake, and even Nipissing, Ontario.

We went with the 700 Club Team to Rapid Lake and Maiganajik. They taped television interviews with me. We handed out backpacks to the school children and they showed a 'Superbook' movie to the children in Rapid Lake as well as Maiganajik.

These communities were touched by the love the 700 Club showed to them. We were all blessed by this visit. What a wonderful ministry this is.

After they left, the Lord set up divine appointments in awesome ways to reach the other areas mentioned. What an awesome God we serve.

The 700 Club was also used by the Lord to bless us with a generator to provide power, a pump, and septic system. We now have running water! Glory be to God. We received food and clothing for the entire community. They demonstrated God's love in action to all. I thank God for His wonderful goodness demonstrated by the 700 Club in Canada. Praise His holy name.

Blessings in a Court House– August 6, 2012

Monday, I had to appear at the court in Maniwaki, Quebec. When I arrived, I met a family of First Nations people from Abitibi in Northern Quebec. We arrived at the same time and I asked them if they had any school-aged children. There were many backpacks left. They had six children. I gave them six backpacks and told them these were from the 700 Club. They were joyful to receive them. Imagine being blessed at court. Only God can set this up.

Those waiting to appear in the courtroom were given numbers. My number was 56. I was also born in '56. While we sat in the waiting area, a lawyer came out and announced, in a loud voice, that the Poucachiche family's case was dismissed. This was the same family that I had given the backpacks to. They were told to meet with this lawyer in a side room so he could explain why the case was dismissed. Wow, the Lord is so awesome. They were truly blessed and joyful.

Then a lady walked over and sat beside me. She poured out her heart to me. She told me that she was a believer and that she had done wrong. She was taking full responsibility for her actions. She was confessing all of this to me. I told her that it would be wonderful if the court would be as forgiving as our Lord. She asked, "What do you mean?" I told her that because we are believers, we can confess our sins and be forgiven and the Lord remembers them no more.

We were called into the courtroom. The same police officer who accompanied us on our visit to Rapid Lake was sitting at the front. He seemed quite surprised to see me walk into the courtroom.

When they finally called my number, I walked to the stand in front of the judge. The prosecutor stood up and said, "We are sorry, Madame, there has been an error. There are no charges against you. You can go."

I thanked him and turned to go. I noticed the woman I had spoken to about the Father's forgiveness. She had a beaming smile. She gave me a 'thumbs up' as I walked past her.

Letter to 700 Club Canada - July 2012

Enjoying ice cream with the children from Maiganajik

Your message came in at the perfect time. I was just driving in to the Domaine when I received your text message. Your rooms have been booked for the 3rd and 4th of August.

While driving, I had a phone call from Pastor Mark Redner. Mark is the pastor at the West Carleton Christian Assembly, in Kinburn, Ontario. He called to pray with me over the telephone. What a blessing to have encouragement like this. The Lord is awesome and the timing perfect.

One of the children in the photo, the one standing up in the middle of the photo, was healed just hours before this photo was taken. Her little brother, the little boy on the far left, carried her into the cabin.

She had fallen off her bicycle and couldn't walk. All of the children in the photo were there. The little girl, fourth from the left, had just told me that she did not believe in Jesus because someone had told her that it was not true.

The little boy placed his little sister on the sofa. I looked at the little girl who didn't believe. I told her that I was going to ask Jesus to heal her sister and she would see that Jesus is real and that He answers when we pray.

I put my hands on the little girl's foot, and told her that I was going to ask Jesus to heal her. I told her that Jesus would take all the pain away, too. I told her to close her eyes and think about Jesus.

I prayed, and with my hands still on her foot, I asked her if she felt warm anywhere. She said yes. She told me that it was warm further up her leg. She pointed to just below the knee. I told her that Jesus was healing her and that was why she felt the warmth.

She began to smile, a real big smile. I knew she was healed. I took my hands away and she stood up. She seemed a little unsure at first. When she realized that there was no pain, she walked, then she ran. We watched as she put all of her weight on the leg that was healed, and she jumped up on a chair. Praise be to God.

A little later in the day, the sister who said she didn't believe asked me to pray and ask Jesus to heal her toe! Praise God, I did, and the Lord healed her toe. She now knows that Jesus is real.

A lady and a man came in the afternoon for prayer. The Lord healed them also. What a wonderful Lord we serve. It is awesome to pray for the sick and witness the healing power of God. I get to proclaim the Gospel when I pray in the name of Jesus. Praise God for these marvelous opportunities.

We had beautiful weather. It was so awesome to spend time with these precious people. I told them that you were planning to come for a visit in August and they are all very happy about that.

I also went to Rapid Lake and the timing was perfect. I arrived just before a bus came to take the Rapid Lake children to an event in Maniwaki.

I was able to hug, kiss, and tell them I love and missed them. It was wonderful to see them all come running to greet me. They recognized me at once. Wow, the Lord is so good. I haven't seen most of these children for two years.

I tried to find George Nottaway while I was in Rapid Lake, but did not find him. I met George in Rapid Lake in 2008. George is a Christian brother who had been praying for his village most of his life. He had a vision of the Lord Jesus when he was only seven years old. George has a wonderful heart full of compassion for his people. George has encouraged and supported me in this work and I thank God for him.

Late last night, George came to the cabin in Maiganajik and we prayed for him. What a wonderful blessing to see him. George is staying in Maiganajik now and wants to have Bible study in his home. Praise God.

I look forward to finally meeting you in person. I feel like an excited little child getting ready to meet my sister. Glory be to God. It's amazing how the Lord fills our hearts with love for one another and we haven't even met each other yet. The Lord is amazing, what awesome love. Praise His holy name.

700 Club Canada TV Crew in Rapid Lake and Maiganajik

Two of the 700 Club Canada interviews filmed in Rapid Lake were aired on television October 25th, 2012. The interview filmed in Maiganajik was aired on television November 26th, 2012. These interviews are available for public viewing on the 700Club.ca website and can be found in the video archives.

Chapter 7

My Best Friend Can Be Your Best Friend Too

Psalm 32:1-5
Oh, what joy for those whose disobedience is forgiven,
Whose sin is put out of sight!
Yes, what joy for those whose record the Lord has cleared
of guilt,
Whose lives are lived in complete honesty!
When I refused to confess my sin,
My body wasted away and I groaned all day long.
Day and night your hand of discipline was heavy on me.
My strength evaporated like water in the summer heat.
Finally, I confessed all my sins to you and stopped trying to
hide my guilt.
I said to myself, "I will confess my rebellion to the Lord."
And you forgave me! All my guilt is gone.

My Best Friend Can Be Your Best Friend Too!
Do you ever feel afraid or lonely or think that nobody really knows you or that no one really cares about you? I used to feel this way, but I heard a wonderful secret one day when I was about nine years old. This secret changed my whole life.

I found out that somebody does understand me, cares about me and loves me more than I ever dreamed possible, and keeps me safe, so I don't need to be afraid of anyone or anything ever. That somebody is Jesus, the Son of the living God.

I was so excited when I heard about Jesus, and especially when I found out that He is alive and loves me. He loves you, too! Isn't that absolutely awesome?

You can know Jesus and He can be your best friend too. He loves everyone, and especially children. Jesus changed my whole life. I talk to Him about everything and He loves me and understands me completely. I don't know if you ever heard about Jesus before, maybe you have, but did you know that He is alive and wants you to know Him, I mean really know Him?

Jesus Christ is the Son of the one true living God. Everything that we see and don't see was made by God, through Jesus and for Jesus. One day Jesus came to this earth and lived here. God sent Him to rescue us because we were in big trouble. Sin took us away from God and we needed someone to bring us back to God.

Jesus was born into this world by a young woman named Mary and by the Holy Spirit, not by a man but by the Spirit of God, because God is His father. Jesus came and lived here in a body just like ours, but He was not like us because God lived in Him. Jesus came to tell us about God and to show us how to get back to God and go to heaven when we leave this earth.

Jesus is the only way to get back to God. We can only come to God through Jesus, God's Son. By believing that Jesus is the Son of God, that He was born into this world and lived here, that He did die for us and that God raised Him back to life again by the power of the Holy Spirit, we can ask Him to come and live in our hearts and make us right with God and have eternal life.

People didn't realize that Jesus was the Son of God, and they killed Him by putting Him on a cross, but what they didn't know was that God had already planned that Jesus would die for us. He gave up His own life for us.

Believing in Him and what He did, we would not have to die. That's how much He loves us. Isn't that wonderful? Jesus took the punishment for all the terrible things that we did so we could be made right with God and live forever with Him and not have to die.

He didn't stay dead, because God raised Him back to life by the power of the Holy Spirit. Isn't that amazing? When we believe in Jesus and what He did for us, we can ask Jesus to come and live in our hearts, and we can ask God to give us the Holy Spirit to come and help us and give us a new life that never ends—and He will. All we have to do is ask Him.

God, the creator of all things, gave all power and authority to Jesus and now Jesus is alive and Lord of everything and everyone. He also wants you to know Him. He is the only one who really knows God the Father, and He wants us to know God too. When we believe this, we also become children of God.

It's important to have the Holy Spirit because it's the Holy Spirit who actually comes to live inside us, and He teaches us all about Jesus. The Holy Spirit is the Spirit of Jesus and also the Spirit of God, too. He is the one Jesus will send to help us, and the awesome thing is, He will never leave us. He keeps us safe and lets us know that God loves us. He is awesome, the greatest friend anyone could ever have.

The Holy Spirit knows everything about everything and tells us wonderful secrets about Jesus, God, and everything else, too.

I hope that you will become a child of God like me, and have the awesome life that He gives. There is no one else like Him and there is nothing greater than being a child of God.

If you are not sure how to ask Jesus to come into your life, pray this prayer out loud, from your heart, and ask Jesus to come into your heart:

Heavenly Father, I want to know You. I come to You admitting that I am a sinner. Right now, I choose to turn away from sin, and I ask You to forgive me and cleanse me of all unrighteousness. Jesus, I believe that You are the Son of God and that You came to live on earth in a human body. I believe that You died on the cross and were buried for me and that You took the punishment for my sin, so I could be forgiven and made right with God and have eternal life through You. I believe that God raised You from the dead by the power of the Holy Spirit and that You are alive and that You are Lord. I ask You, Lord Jesus, to come into my heart and be my Lord and give me the desire and power to live for You. I call upon the name of Jesus Christ to be the Savior and Lord of my life. Jesus, I choose to follow You and ask to be born again by the power of the Holy Spirit. I ask You to teach me, lead me, and guide me. I declare that right now, I am a child of God. I am free from sin and full of the righteousness of God in Christ Jesus my Lord. I am saved in Jesus' name. Amen.

The Holy Spirit will help you to understand what is written here.

Did you ask God to make you His own child by asking Jesus to come into your heart? If you did, then welcome to the family of God, you are now a child of God and Jesus lives in your heart.

You have just made the greatest decision of your entire life. Be ready for your life to change. It will change and you will have awesome joy in your precious heart, because that's just one of the awesome things Jesus will give you.

I am so excited for you. If I were there, I would give you a great big hug, but I'm not, so I will ask the Lord to give you one for me. I know that He will. You may not see Him, but you will feel Him and His wonderful love. He is going to fill your precious heart with His love.

Remember to tell someone that Jesus is your Lord and that you are a believer in Jesus. This is very important.

Tell others about the wonderful things that Jesus is doing in your life. This pleases Him very much and it helps others to know Him, too. We want everyone to know how awesome Jesus is and that they can know Him, too.

Now you will never be alone again, not ever! Isn't it wonderful to know that the God who made the whole universe and everything in it, is now your Father? He will be with you ALWAYS and He will never leave you or give you up.

The Holy Spirit will lead and guide you, teach you all things, comfort you, help you and tell you about things to come. He will tell you all about Jesus and God, and you can ask Him anything and He will help you.

When you talk to Him, it's called "praying." That's what we do, we talk to Him and He talks to us. He talks to us "inside." You can talk to Him like a best friend and He will never ever hurt you. He is love, and that's what He does.

There is so much to know about Him. One of the first things that you will notice is that He changes you on the inside. You will feel different, you will love more, laugh more, and care about others more. Here are some of the things that you will notice inside you now that the Holy Spirit lives in you: Love, Joy, Peace, Patience, Kindness, Gentleness, Faithfulness, Goodness, and Self-Control.

The Holy Spirit also gives us a "new language." It might sound weird and you won't know what you are saying, but it is a language that God understands. When you start speaking this language, it's because the Holy Spirit inside you is praying for you to God. This is really amazing. When I started speaking this new language, I didn't know what it was. I woke up in the middle of the night, speaking a strange language. Now I know and I thank God for it.

It's so wonderful to be able to speak to God in another language and know that He is the only one who understands it. It is very special. I can do it any time I want to, and so can you. Especially, when we don't know what to say or ask Him for. I just speak in the new language that He gave me. It's called "tongues" in the Bible.

If you have a Bible at home, the Holy Spirit will also help you understand it. Ask Him, and He will teach it to you. He is the One who gave the information in the Bible to the people who wrote it, so He is the only one who can really help you to understand it. Remember, you are a child of God and Christ (Jesus) lives in you. You are part of another family now, and you have many brothers and sisters "in Christ," and I am one of them. One day I will see you in heaven. I love you.

I would like to pray for you:

Father, I thank You for the precious one reading this. I ask You to teach them Your word by Your Holy Spirit and I ask that they experience the love of Christ Jesus. I ask You to keep them safe, Father, and let them know how much You love them. In the name of Jesus I pray, Amen.

Chapter 8

Scripture Verses from the Bible (NLT)

Romans 1:1-7
Greetings from Paul
This letter is from Paul, a slave of Christ Jesus, chosen by God to be an apostle and sent out to preach his Good News. God promised this Good News long ago through his prophets in the holy Scriptures. The Good News is about his Son. In his earthly life he was born into King David's family line, and he was shown to be the Son of God when he was raised from the dead by the power of the Holy Spirit. He is Jesus Christ our Lord. Through Christ, God has given us the privilege and authority as apostles to tell Gentiles everywhere what God has done for them, so that they will believe and obey him, bringing glory to his name. And you are included among those Gentiles who have been called to belong to Jesus Christ. I am writing to all of you in Rome who are loved by God and are called to be his own holy people. May God our Father and the Lord Jesus Christ give you grace and peace.

Acts 1:1-5 The Promise of the Holy Spirit
In my first book I told you, Theophilus, about everything Jesus began to do and teach until the day he was taken up to

heaven after giving his chosen apostles further instructions through the Holy Spirit. During the forty days after his crucifixion, he appeared to the apostles from time to time, and he proved to them in many ways that he was actually alive. And he talked to them about the Kingdom of God. Once when he was eating with them, he commanded them, "Do not leave Jerusalem until the Father sends you the gift he promised, as I told you before. John baptized with water, but in just a few days you will be baptized with the Holy Spirit."

1 Corinthians 14:2
For if you have the ability to speak in tongues, you will be talking only to God, since people won't be able to understand you. You will be speaking by the power of the Spirit, but it will all be mysterious.

John 1:1-34
Prologue: Christ, the Eternal Word
In the beginning the Word already existed. The Word was with God, and the Word was God. He existed in the beginning with God. God created everything through him, and nothing was created except through him. The Word gave life to everything that was created, and his life brought light to everyone. The light shines in the darkness, and the darkness can never extinguish it. God sent a man, John the Baptist, to tell about the light so that everyone might believe because of his testimony. John himself was not the light; he was simply a witness to tell about the light. The one who is the true light, who gives light to everyone, was coming into the world. He came into the very world he created, but the world didn't recognize him. He came to his own people, and even they rejected him. But to all who believed him and accepted him, he gave the right to become children of God. They are reborn—not with a physical birth resulting from human passion or plan, but a birth that comes from God.

Scripture Verses from the Bible (NLT)

So the Word became human and made his home among us. He was full of unfailing love and faithfulness. And we have seen his glory, the glory of the Father's one and only Son. John testified about him when he shouted to the crowds, "This is the one I was talking about when I said, 'Someone is coming after me who is far greater than I am, for he existed long before me.'" From his abundance we have all received one gracious blessing after another. For the law was given through Moses, but God's unfailing love and faithfulness came through Jesus Christ. No one has ever seen God. But the unique One, who is himself God, is near to the Father's heart. He has revealed God to us. This was John's testimony when the Jewish leaders sent priests and Temple assistants from Jerusalem to ask John, "Who are you?" He came right out and said, "I am not the Messiah." "Well then, who are you?" they asked. "Are you Elijah?" "No," he replied. "Are you the Prophet we are expecting?" "No." "Then who are you? We need an answer for those who sent us. What do you have to say about yourself?" John replied in the words of the prophet Isaiah: "I am a voice shouting in the wilderness, 'Clear the way for the LORD's coming!'" Then the Pharisees who had been sent asked him, "If you aren't the Messiah or Elijah or the Prophet, what right do you have to baptize?" John told them, "I baptize with water, but right here in the crowd is someone you do not recognize. Though his ministry follows mine, I'm not even worthy to be his slave and untie the straps of his sandal." This encounter took place in Bethany, an area east of the Jordan River, where John was baptizing. The next day John saw Jesus coming toward him and said, "Look! The Lamb of God who takes away the sin of the world! He is the one I was talking about when I said, 'A man is coming after me who is far greater than I am, for he existed long before me.' I did not recognize him as the Messiah, but I have been baptizing with water so that he might be revealed to Israel." Then John testified, "I saw the Holy Spirit descending like a dove from heaven and resting upon him. I didn't know he was the one, but when God sent me to baptize with water, he told me, 'The one on whom you see the Spirit descend and rest is the one who will baptize with the Holy Spirit.' I saw this happen to Jesus, so I testify that he is the Chosen One of God."

John 16:12-15
"There is so much more I want to tell you, but you can't bear it now. When the Spirit of truth comes, he will guide you into all truth. He will not speak on his own but will tell you what he has heard. He will tell you about the future. He will bring me glory by telling you whatever he receives from me. All that belongs to the Father is mine; this is why I said, 'The Spirit will tell you whatever he receives from me.'

The Greatest in the Kingdom – **Luke 9:46-48**
Then his disciples began arguing about which of them was the greatest. But Jesus knew their thoughts, so he brought a little child to his side. Then he said to them, "Anyone who welcomes a little child like this on my behalf welcomes me, and anyone who welcomes me also welcomes my Father who sent me. Whoever is the least among you is the greatest."

About the Author

*B*orn in Shawville, Quebec, Canada on October 16, 1956, Lorraine grew up in the small Western Quebec town of Danford Lake. She has experienced the wonderful goodness of God from childhood. With a passion for others to know and experience the goodness of God through faith in Jesus Christ, Lorraine shares the life-changing message of the Gospel of Jesus Christ and the Kingdom of God. While preparing this book, the Lord spoke to Lorraine, saying, "The Time has come for you to testify."

You will see the power and love of God at work in everyday life.

Discover the life that belongs to you.

The author is an ordinary woman with faith in God.

While writing this book, the Lord softly spoke to Lorraine's heart, saying, "The time has come for you to testify."

Read these amazing testimonies and know that nothing is impossible with God. You will see the amazing love of God in action in everyday life.

The author shows that God is with us at every single moment of the day, in the little things as well as the big things. We often know that in our minds, but depending on our emotions, don't always feel that that is true. With this book, readers will be able to see it's not just something that people tell you at church to encourage attendance of services. God's omnipresent quality is a reality that each one of His children can live out, a truth that doesn't end or change.

Some people believe that God is present, but does not care. This book shows any reader that He intervenes in our lives as our caretaker. The author shows God's character in not only knowing what we need, but also knowing the perfect way to supply the need. This shows He truly is our creator and the source of our lives, not an entity that initiated our existence and then left us to fend for ourselves.

In every story and situation, the author consistently gives glory to God. Because God is such a perfect provider, we can easily forget He is the source of everything good. This book will be a good example and reminder for readers not to take God for granted, but just as He continually provides, we should continually praise.